Copyright © 2024 Naresh

All rights re

The names of some characters portrayed in this book have been changed in order to protect their privacy.

No part of this book may be reproduced, or stored in a retrieval system, or transmitted in any form or by any means, electronic, mechanical, photocopying, recording, or otherwise, without express written permission of the publisher, 2B[red].

2B[red]
because some books deserve to be read
www.2Bred.org

ISBN 978-1-3999-7871-2

Cover design by: 2B[red]
Printed in the United Kingdom

CONTENTS

Copyright
Pink City Kid   1
Preface   2
Chapter 1: How I ended up on the streets   4
Chapter 2: Becoming a slave   29
Chapter 3: The mean old executioner   46
Chapter 4: Getting rid of the lice   71
Chapter 5: The day I nearly died in the holy lake   92
Chapter 6: Kidnapped in Agra   114
Chapter 7: From downward to upward   136
Chapter 8: Making foreign friends   153
Chapter 9: The day the Pink City changed   162
Chapter 10: Little blue house on the edge of the desert   174
Publisher's postscript   177
Acknowledgements   178
About The Author   179

Introduction - A Brief Note From The Editor

I can't imagine how somebody who has never read a book could possibly write one. But Naresh has done just that. He wrote *Pink City Kid* by speaking his story into a mobile phone app while he was locked down in India during the COVID-19 pandemic.

My job was simply to edit the English translation of the narrative into a book form. Contrary to my expectations, I found this surprisingly easy to do. From the outset I decided that I would make no attempt to turn the text into 'literary prose.' I wanted my interventions to be minimal, so it would remain as close as possible to Naresh's authentic spoken voice. This is entirely Naresh's story, told as he would tell it to you sitting in his living room over a cup of *chai*. It's an astonishing feat to recite a book. Very much like the oral tradition of epic story telling that has existed in India for millennia.

It's fascinating to see how Naresh's storytelling style becomes more confident as the book progresses, mirroring his physical growth and the development of his self-confidence in the story. By the middle of the book, when he describes episodes such as the time he almost drowned in the holy lake at Pushkar, or how he was kidnapped in Agra, or how sexual assault was an accepted everyday risk for street kids like him, his voice has matured into that of a skilled storyteller, who peppers the narrative with interesting anecdotes and his own down-to-earth philosophy. I believe the development of his voice is an important element of the authenticity of the book, and I made no attempt to change it.

Why should *Pink City Kid* be published? From the author's point of view, as Naresh states in the book, there are millions of street kids around the world. Nobody ever listens to their voices. So he is speaking as – perhaps – one of their only genuine representatives.

My own opinion, as a representative of **2B[red]**? First, I think the book is an engaging and endearing insight into the humanity of the world's most marginalised people, through the eyes of an innocent but highly intelligent child. It's a great read. It pulls you into a hidden world as the story develops. It's an ultimately uplifting tale, filled with fascinating facts and anecdotes. But there's a more profound reason, which I'd like to illustrate with a small, personal story of my own.

Last year I was sitting on a sunny terrace in Athens, drinking a late-afternoon glass of wine, and editing the latest section of *Pink City Kid* on my laptop. I watched a skinny little boy going from table to table, attempting to sell a small packet of paper handkerchiefs. I could tell from his body language, from the wary distance he kept from people, that he was familiar with the very worst side of humanity. I have seen this kid – boys and girls – many times before in many countries. They buy some packs of tissues at 10 cents each, and attempt to sell them for 20 cents, happy if, at the end of a long day of work, they have earned a euro. I watched the boy in Athens being ignored by people, or snarled and shouted at, or rudely shooed away.

When the boy arrived at my table, I handed him 5 euros for his pack of tissues and raised my hand to indicate that I wanted no change. He was immensely polite, that ragged little boy. He clasped the banknote to his heart, and said, "efharisto." As I looked into his eyes, I saw the child in *Pink City Kid* looking back. For weeks afterwards, I struggled to rid myself of what I saw in that little kid's eyes: that brief glimpse into the horror of his existence; things you should never see in the eyes of a child.

Sitting there, enjoying my privileged position in the world, I wondered if a reading of Naresh's book might have changed the responses of some of those folk on that Athens terrace. Could a reading of *Pink City Kid* have humanized the poor Greek boy? Could it have revealed him to be a vulnerable human being, with feelings and emotions, worthy of being treated with a little human kindness? I think so. And that's one of the overriding reasons why I, and 2B[red], believe that Naresh's book needs to be published. Poverty-ism is perhaps the last great 'ism' that we need to recognize in ourselves. Little Naresh is still to be found, everywhere around us, wandering the streets of our great cities, barefoot and ragged.

    2B[red] is proud to publish a book that we feel needed to be written and needs to be read. If you enjoy reading *Pink City Kid*, if you find some value in it, please pass your copy on to others. If you know anybody who might be interested in it, please spread the word. If you are a member of a book club, please suggest it for collective reading. If you are a TikTokker, please give your opinion. And please do leave a review of it somewhere on-line. Your help could make a real difference for street kids all over the world.

PJ, Publishing Editor, 2B[red]

Pink City Kid
My life as a street child in India

By Naresh Kishwani

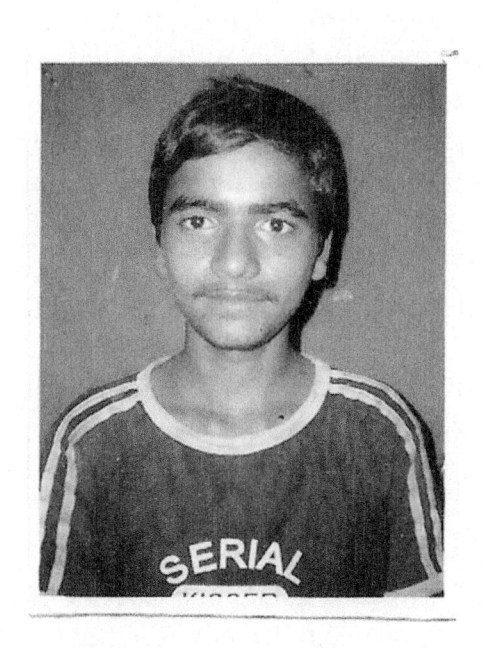

Preface

How to write a book if you can hardly read or write

I've never written anything before in my life, not even a story at school. You see, I grew up as a street kid, so I didn't go to school. In fact, I'm not really writing this at all. I'm speaking it to you. I'm speaking into an app on my mobile phone. When I'm happy with what I've recorded, I WhatsApp the file it to my friend Shiba. She listens to my voice and writes it down. Then she makes photos of the pages and sends them to Sunita. She types them into her computer and translates them into English, because I'm speaking to you in Hindi. I've never read a book, so I don't know if this will become one in the end. Let's see.

I want to tell you about my life when I was a kid. It's not such an unusual story. It's just like the story of millions of kids around the world who live on the streets. Sometimes they live as slaves. Like I did for a while. They're often abused and treated like they're worthless. Just as I was. Nobody listened to me then. And nobody is listening to those kids right now. So I want to speak for them.

First, let me tell you where *you* are. You're sitting in my house, on the edge of the desert, just outside the Indian city of Jaipur. It's a summer afternoon, so it's too hot to be outdoors. But I have an electric *punkah,* and it's blowing a nice cool breeze onto us.

Let me begin ...

PINK CITY KID

Chapter 1: How I ended up on the streets

There are lots of ways you can end up living as a street kid in India. Each little kid has their own little story. I've heard so many of them over the years. There are *lakhs* of different stories – at least one story for every god in the whole of the country.

Some kids were born on the street and have always lived there with their families. Some were abandoned as infants. Left at the side of the road because their parents couldn't afford to feed them, or they had died. Often they don't remember their parents at all. Sometimes they don't even know their real name, they just have a nickname that they were given by somebody. If you think I'm exaggerating about that, I've got something to tell you later-on that might shock you. Many street kids escaped from slavery. There are many types of slavery. I know how it is to live as a slave. I can also tell you about that, if you want to hear it. Others kids escaped from abusive families or orphanages. Some have no idea how they ended up living on the street. Looking after themselves – surviving – that's all they remember ever doing.

So there are many different ways you can end up being a street kid in India. I don't recommend you try any of them. But let me tell you my own little story of how I became homeless, and lived for many years on the streets of Jaipur, the Pink City of Rajasthan.

❖ ❖ ❖

My name is Naresh. I wasn't born on the street. My family was never rich, but my grandfather – my papa's father, that is – had a *chai* stall in Ajmer. He also owned his own house there, so he had done pretty well for himself. Ajmer is a town in the northern Indian state of Rajasthan. It's beautiful there. The beauty is free for everyone to enjoy, rich and poor. You can always see the mountains, and there's a huge lake.

I guess things started to go really wrong for us after my mom died. That happened when I was about one-and-a-half, or so I'm told. I'm not sure exactly how old I was then, as I'm not sure how old I am now. My papa didn't remember the date of my birthday. Not even the year. He tells me I'm about 4 or 5 years younger than Raji, my sister, but he doesn't remember her birthday either, so nothing is certain. The alcohol didn't help his memory.

My mom had been suffering from TB for years. Even back in the 1990s it could be cured if you had a lot of money to pay for the treatment. We didn't. Poor people still die of it today in India. My cousin's fiancée died of TB just a couple of years ago. She was only twenty years old, and this is the twenty-first century.

Before I was born, the work situation became pretty bad in Ajmer. Lots of people were unemployed and it was difficult to survive. My grandfather was growing old, and so he decided to sell his property to give his two sons a start in life. He rented a place to live, and sold the family house for only 40,000 rupees. That's about 550 US dollars now. Even then it wasn't a lot of money. My grandfather gave half of it to my papa and half to my uncle. His intention was good, but it wasn't a smart thing to do. Having somewhere to live is what's most important.

When he received his portion of the money, my papa brought my mom and my sister to Jaipur – the Rajasthan state capital – in search of work. His big plan was to buy a second-hand taxi, which he would drive in Jaipur to earn a living. But he didn't do that. Instead he started to drive a rented cycle-rickshaw, and he also rented a home for us. When you look back, you can see where the mistakes were made. You can see how that 20,000 rupees could have been used better. I guess my papa thought he would save it for a while.

All went well in Jaipur for a few months, but then one day a letter arrived saying my grandfather's health was bad and everyone had to come back home to Ajmer. My papa locked the family possessions in our rented house – all the things they had brought with them to Jaipur – and he went back to Ajmer with my mom and my sister, and me too in a way. By then my mom was pregnant with me.

Grandfather was admitted to hospital and he was treated for a few weeks. But he passed away. Nobody knew what was actually wrong with him. Old age, they said.

Some of my papa's money had been spent on grandfather's treatment, and then more on the funeral and all the Hindu rituals that go on for weeks afterwards. It's really expensive to die in India. After that, my parents stayed in Ajmer for a few more months, and during that period I was born there.

Shortly after my birth, my papa's younger brother was also found dead one day. Nobody was really sure why he had died, because he was only in his twenties at the time. But nobody was really surprised either. It was most likely from an overdose. He had been a drug addict and an alcoholic for years. By then his 20,000 rupees had already been wasted on his addictions. My grandfather should have known better than to give money to him. He did nothing positive with it, just used it to kill himself. He used to inject heroin. When he didn't have the money to buy heroin, he used to drink *doda*. That's a green drink made from dried poppy heads that they grind up and mix with boiling water. It's illegal now, but it's still easy to buy, and very cheap.

So then there was another expensive funeral and those endless rituals, which my papa had to pay for as well. You could say that my uncle not only wasted his share of the money on drink and drugs, but by killing himself, he took what was left of my papa's share too. In the space of about one year, all the money from the sale of the family home was gone. Spent on hospitals, drugs, drink, and funerals. My grandfather had worked hard all his life to buy that house for his family, and he left my grandmother living in a rented room with no income.

Almost immediately after my uncle's death, his wife – my *chacchi* – married a wealthy man who owned a textile shop. She had a little boy and a girl to look after, and no money, so I think she was afraid. She just disappeared one day with her kids, without telling anybody in the family that they were leaving. I guess she already knew the man before my uncle died.

When the mourning rituals were over, my papa returned to Jaipur, but with a bigger family this time. My mom, my sister Raji, me, and my grandmother. We couldn't go back to our previous rented house, where all our possessions had been locked inside, because the rent was due for many months, and my papa couldn't pay such a huge amount. He was broke. So he rented a single room in another part of the city, and the five of us moved-in there.

It was OK for a while. But in those days it seems that things didn't stay OK for very long. Next, my mom's health started getting worse due to her TB. So my papa got my mom admitted to a free government hospital in Jaipur. He had a lot of responsibilities, and they started to get on top of him. He was really unhappy because his father and brother had both died, and then my mom's health was becoming serious and it was difficult to take care of her. All the funds were gone, and we had no relatives who were willing to support or help us.

My papa was at the hospital every day, trying to arrange for medicine and get the doctors to treat my mom. But it was useless. There was no treatment for TB unless you were rich. You needed to rest and take expensive drugs for months, maybe even for a year. Then my mom's health became severe. She started coughing-up blood and got so weak that she passed away after just a short stay in hospital. But my mom didn't really die of TB. She died from being poor.

It's not really surprising that my papa became depressed after my mom's death. I heard this from other relatives. It was like he gave up. Everything seemed to be going wrong in his life. He had to support us kids and now my grandmother too. My grandmother couldn't even help looking after us. She was so old she could hardly walk. In fact, my papa had to carry her in his arms when she wanted to use the bathroom. He also had big debts, and had to pay rent for his cycle-rickshaw and our room before we could even think about eating.

It was around that time that he started drinking really heavily. He stopped paying the rent on our room, and my grandmother argued constantly with him about that. And she couldn't tolerate his drinking. After all, her other son had just died from drink and drugs. Eventually she decided to move back to Ajmer to live with my *bua*. That's my papa's younger sister. In India we have names for all those different types of relatives.

With my grandmother gone, there were just the three of us. I was a toddler of 2 or 3 years, and my sister was just a few years older, but my papa had to leave us alone in the house all day in order to work. There was no choice.

He really did his best. After we had a breakfast of *chai*, biscuits, and milk, early in the morning he would cycle his rickshaw to earn some cash, and he would bring us lunch if he had been lucky enough to have any customers. Then he would go back to work.

With his earnings for the day he would bring home food to cook in the evening, plus wine for himself. He would always start to drink while he was cooking. Who could really blame him? His life must have felt like a nightmare, living hand to mouth, with increasing debts, and no way out.

But things improved. As my papa became known in the neighbourhood, he got to know all the shop owners in the textile market and they grew to trust him. He used to transport clothes and textiles on his rickshaw from the factories on the outskirts of Jaipur to their shops in the Pink City. He had regular work then, and close to our home. Sometimes he even brought home clothes for us that had been rejected by the shops. So our life got better for a while, and we were living happily there, just the three of us.

Perhaps you don't know this. But the old walled city of Jaipur, where we lived, is called the Pink City. All the buildings, and even the wall around the city, are painted pink. They say it was to welcome some English king a long time ago. There really is a high wall around the Pink City. You have to go through one of the gates to get inside. But outside of the wall is the modern city of Jaipur. It's quite small really. It only has about 3 million people.

I have some nice memories of those times. When papa was transporting cloth for the textile factories, he would have a sack of it on the back of his rickshaw like a big soft cushion. He would let my sister and I sit on the top of it and he'd take us with him on his deliveries. We both loved that. Then sometimes we would stop off for delicious street food like, *dahi vada*, which are fried lentil fritters served with yoghurt and spicy chutney. Or maybe we would stop at *dhaba* to eat egg curry, *muttar* goat curry, or my favourite, *aloo tikki* potatoes. Perhaps you already know this, but a *dhaba* is a simple restaurant at the side of the road. They are everywhere in India. The food is very cheap, but it can be better than the food at a real restaurant if it's a good *dhaba*. They cook big steel pots of food, and they are constantly making fresh *roti*. Some of them are always open, day and night. You can usually sit outside in Rajasthan because for most of the year it never rains.

Our room was in the Muslim colony. We were the only Hindus living there at the time. It was really nice. The rent was low and the people were friendly. But it was pretty dirty. The streets were narrow and on a steep slope. Every morning, people would throw the garbage out of their houses into the street. Nobody had water in their home, so early morning, people would fill buckets with water from a standpipe in the street. Lots got spilled and it was very messy. Also, most people had a goat. They were allowed to roam free in the neighbourhood during the day. But at night they would all return home to be fed, and they would be tied-up outside the houses. So there was always the smell of goats and lots of goat shit everywhere.

Life was never boring in the Muslim colony. There were always arguments in the street about parking motor bikes, or noise, or something small. Lots of yelling and swearing. Often people would slap one another, but not seriously. Like the way little children fight. Nobody really got hurt and it was always funny to watch. They didn't behave like Hindus usually do. They were interesting. And there were lots of noisy Muslim kids in the neighbourhood. I had plenty of friends.

Things were going really well, and we were very happy living together in the Muslim colony. We used to have fun in that little room. We had no TV, but we would play games or talk in the evenings. Life is often good until other people interfere.

Then one day, out of the blue, a distant cousin came to find us. I'm not sure what the Hindi name for that relative is. He said he needed my papa's help because his father-in-law was suffering from cancer and he was in the hospital. They needed somebody who could be there 24-7 to wash him and take care of him. There were no nurses. So for some reason he came looking for my papa. I'm not sure why, but it needed to be a man because a woman who was not his wife or daughter wouldn't be allowed to stay with him. His wife was dead and I suppose his daughter didn't want to look after him.

So he asked my papa for help, and in return he promised that my sister and I could stay at his house. He said, "My mother and my wife are always at home. They can take care of your kids better than you can. And we can send them to a private school so that they can study. They'll have good food and a good upbringing."

To my papa it sounded like a big opportunity. His kids would have a future. They would go to school and get an education. They would have home-cooked food every day, and new clothes when they needed them. So he said yes.

Of course, my sister and I were both dead against it. We refused at first, but he said, "It's a great chance for you both. You'll have a better life if you go and stay there." Eventually, we had no choice but to agree. So we vacated our rented room in the Muslim colony and we moved the very next day to that person's home. My papa went to stay at the hospital, taking care of my cousin's father-in-law.

At the start, my cousin's wife and his mother were OK with us. We called his mother 'Aunty.' She ruled the household. But she wasn't really our aunty. Nor was my cousin a real cousin. They were only related by marriage to my *bua*.

Of course, we quickly realised that all the promises they made were false. Although our names were registered at a private school as they said, we were never allowed to go. Private schools cost a lot of money.

After few weeks the old man in hospital died. His body was brought home and there was another funeral, and yet more rituals continuing for ten or fifteen days. From that point, my papa was free from his side of the agreement, but he didn't come and collect us as we hoped. He said, "You both stay here for a little while longer. Now I have no room, no home to take you too. But I'll cycle the rickshaw, and sleep where I can in the street to save money. When I've saved enough, I'll get a rented place, and then I'll take you back." We believed him, of course. In a way he must have been relieved not to have to work, and pay bills, and look after two young kids at the same time.

So my papa started paying 50 rupees a day for Aunty to keep us, sometimes 20 or 30 rupees more if there were extra expenses, and he started to sleep on the sidewalk next to his cycle-rickshaw to save money.

Often he would visit us at night, bringing things like chocolate or ice cream. My cousin's family didn't like that because he didn't bring things for them. So they became jealous of us and angry with my papa. But we always shared what we had with them.

As time went by, my papa's visits became less frequent. The gaps between them got bigger. Sometimes it was a week or two weeks, and then a month. When he would come to see us, he was often really drunk. Aunty used to shout at him about not bringing enough money, so his visits got even less frequent.

Each time we saw him he would say the same thing: "I'll save some money and then I'll rent a home and take you back." But he was never able to save enough. I don't know why. I think he also owed a lot of rent for the cycle-rickshaw. Perhaps he spent too much on drink. It went on like this for months.

When he stopped paying money to Aunty completely, her behaviour towards us changed. She obviously thought: I'm not going to feed them for free, so why not make them work for us.

She arranged for me to work on a vegetable cart. I suppose I was about six years of age. I would leave the house early in the morning, around 7 a.m., and I used to get back to Aunty's house about 4 or 5 p.m. I spent the whole day working. I used to take care of the cart, and walk around the colony on foot doing odd jobs while the owner sold his vegetables door-to-door. For my work, he used to give 15 rupees directly to Aunty. My sister was made to do all her household work, like mopping, sweeping up, and washing the dishes.

We were just young kids, and we were trapped. What could we do? Where could we go? So we just put up with it. There was no choice. We even got used to all their bad behaviour, and sometimes it was pretty awful.

All evening my cousin and Aunty used to gamble. They would go to bed very late at night. Many people used to come to gamble in the house and they would drink a lot of alcohol. They would play three-card stud or rummy. Aunty's house was very small. It had just two rooms and a small kitchen. My sister and I slept on the floor in the main room of the house, where they played cards. So we couldn't go to bed until late at night, when everyone had gone home.

◆ ◆ ◆

Sometimes I used to miss our old life in the Muslim colony. So I would go there on foot now and then after work. It was about 2 or 3 kilometres away from Aunty's house. I didn't have any shoes in those days, but my feet were very tough from walking next to the vegetable cart.

When we lived in the Muslim colony we used to have a puppy. We called him Yellow Dog. You can guess why. He wasn't really ours. He was a street dog. But we used to feed him and give him biscuits. He used to sleep at our home sometimes. Yellow Dog was quite grown up by the time we moved to Aunty's house.

When I would go to visit the Muslim colony, Yellow Dog would recognise me, and he was always happy to see me. I used to take a biscuit or something for him if I could. Then one day he changed. When I went to stroke him in the street he became angry, barking and snarling at me. I'd never seen him act like that before. It was like he had gone crazy. He had always been such a sweet dog.

When I walked away, he ran at me and bit me on the bum. He was young and he had sharp teeth. He tore my only pair of shorts. One of my friends from the colony ran to tell Aunty what had happened. And one of our old Muslim neighbours chased Yellow Dog away with a walking stick and picked me up. I was covered in blood.

So I was taken to a government hospital where they cleaned the bite wound and bandaged me. They gave me some injections. And I had to go back to the hospital for an injection every day for the next two weeks. They said it was very important and that I would die if I didn't go.

When I got back, Aunty told me it was my own fault for approaching a street dog. She wasn't sorry for me at all, and she wouldn't let me stay off work. She wanted her fifteen rupees. So at 7 a.m. I was back walking next to the vegetable cart.

The pain got better after a couple of days, and I wanted to show my friends in the Muslim colony that I was OK. So when I finished work at 5 p.m., I walked back to the colony. It was a big mistake. Yellow Dog was standing waiting for me in the street looking even crazier than last time. There was spit dripping from his mouth. I tried to get away but he ran at me and bit me again, but on the other side of my bum this time. So I was bleeding as badly as before.

A shopkeeper took me to be treated at the hospital again. My shorts were completely ruined this time. The injections and bandages continued each day, but still I had to go to work. I was terrified going to the hospital. When I had only been bitten once, they stuck the needle in the other side of my bum. Now, both sides were very sore, but they still needed to give me an injection every day. I'm still terrified of needles. And dogs.

A few days later, I heard that Yellow Dog had bitten some other kids, and was always having fights with dogs in the street. He had an infected cut on his neck where he had been bitten in a fight. When street dogs get bitten on their neck they usually die. They can lick a bite on their leg to keep it clean, but they can't lick their own neck.

Poor Yellow Dog had become too dangerous, so the men from the colony got together and killed him. Although I couldn't sit down for weeks, I was really sad when I heard that. When we used to live in the Muslim colony we loved Yellow Dog and he loved us. He was such a well-behaved puppy. He used to follow us around and sleep in our home. When we were eating he would sit calmly next to us and we would give him food. One day, he just suddenly went mad. I never knew how or why.

◆ ◆ ◆

There was a *shaadi ka garden* – a marriage garden – near to Aunty's house. If you have never been to Rajasthan, you may not know what that is. It's a big space, like a small park, with a fence or wall around it. During the marriage season, people hold their wedding celebrations there in the evening when it's cooler. It's usually too hot to do it indoors. There is always a big stage and lots of comfortable seats. Everywhere there are balloons and coloured slingers and drapes. The floor is usually covered with bright green cloth that looks like a lawn and has a strange smell. It's too dry in Rajasthan for real grass to grow very easily. They have big kitchens and long rows of tables covered with coloured tablecloths where you can collect all kinds of fantastic food for free. As soon as one dish of food is empty, it gets replaced with a new one. When you get married, you have to invite hundreds of people, and you have to be very generous to them. It's really expensive. A wedding in Rajasthan is even more expensive than a funeral.

At the marriage garden near to Aunty's house, there used to be three or four weddings every week, and sometimes other celebrations for special birthdays and things. Always loud music with people dancing and having fun. And always lots of nice food.

Some of the kids from my colony realised that if they put on their best clean clothes they could sneak into the marriage garden and have dinner there. There were so many people, and so many kids with them, that nobody noticed. There were three gates to enter the marriage garden, but the one near to the stage, that wasn't used, had a gap beneath it. It was easy for a little kid to get under. After they had eaten, they used to collect some plates of food behind the stage and pass them under the gate to their friends. So they would all carry plates of food home to their families.

The next day, in the morning, the ladies from the colony used to stand out in the street discussing what they had last night for dinner from the marriage garden. They used to tell Aunty all about the delicious things their children had brought home for them.

Aunty was quite a jealous lady, and she said to me, "You

should go and have your dinner there, and bring some food home for us too, like the other kids do." She said she would wash my clothes and have them ready for when I returned from work so that I would look neat and tidy. She told my sister to go as well.

So we started going with the other kids, who were all my friends by then. We used to follow the same procedure of bringing plates filled with *gulab jamoon, dahi vada, paneer, ras malai, roti*, and *naan* back to Aunty's house. Aunty was fond of spicy food, so we always tried to bring the hot things like *aluu tikki* to make her happy. Sometimes she didn't cook for days when there were regular events at the marriage garden.

There were four other marriage gardens within just a few kilometres. So if nothing was happening at our own garden, we used to visit those instead. We got really expert at it. We used to go by bicycle in the early evening to see which venue was making preparations. Some of my friends had bikes, and I would sit on the back of one of them. Sometimes we would make a plan to visit two or three on the same evening and have lot of different food to eat. It could be really difficult to get plates of food out of some of them. They had better fences, and they had security guards at the gates, but we did manage sometimes. Whenever I didn't bring anything for Aunty and her daughter-in-law, she used to scold me. She told me I was only allowed to go to our own marriage garden where it was easy to get food out. But I still used to go with my friend. When Aunty wouldn't wash my clothes, my friend used to lend me his nice clothes to wear. So we used to go at 9 or 10 p.m., and after we had eaten, we would return at 11 or 11:30. At Aunty's house they would be busy gambling, and would have drunk a lot by then, so usually nobody would notice.

Many of my friends didn't go daily, but my best friend and I used to always go. We were never hungry in those days. A couple of times we almost got caught, but it was easy to run faster than the security guards. Usually, we just acted like we were invited. We would walk in behind a family with lots of kids, and nobody noticed. This went on for months, and sometimes my sister Raji came along to eat dinner with us. By then there were piles of plates from the wedding garden at Aunty's house. Maybe even a couple of hundred.

❖ ❖ ❖

Then it all started getting worse. Gamblers always lose eventually, and things went wrong for my cousin and Aunty. They built up big gambling debts. They borrowed more money to try to win it back. The harder they tried to win, the more they lost, and the bigger the debts got. People would come and bang on the door asking my cousin for money he owed them. There would be shouting and fights almost every day. My sister and I always got really upset when that happened. We were just little kids. But at least the gambling stopped for a while because nobody trusted them to pay up when they lost.

Then, suddenly one day, we left the house and never went back. We moved to the other side of Jaipur, about ten or twelve kilometres away. I heard about the reason later. The residents of the colony were always protesting to the landlord about the noise. It used to go on until late at night. At all hours there would be people coming to gamble and drink alcohol. The landlord also used to complain whenever he came to collect the rent, but he was helpless. When he told Aunty she had to vacate the house, her family threatened him. They said they would beat-up him and his family if he bothered her again. Aunty told the landlord, "If you want us to leave, you'll need to pay us to go." He had had enough of her, so he paid her thousands of rupees to leave, even though Aunty still owed him a lot of rent.

In a way, it was good for me, because I stopped having to go to work for a while. It was much too far to walk and far too expensive to go by bus. But for a time we had no clue where our papa was, and he didn't even know we had moved house. The last time we had seen him he told us the same old story about saving money and renting a place so that we could live happily together again. I know it was difficult for him to earn much with his rickshaw. And most of what he earned he spent on food and alcohol.

When my papa visited, he would always pay money to Aunty. Sometimes he would also give some money to us, but Aunty used to take that from us when he left. We never dared to tell him about that because we knew we would be left alone with her afterwards. She had a very bad temper.

◆ ◆ ◆

Not having to work didn't last very long. One day Aunty told me I had to find a job and bring in some money. She said, "We've got problems and we're in debt. How do you expect us to support you and your sister when your father doesn't give us any money?" So I had a variety of jobs. None of them lasted more than a few days. I was too young and people didn't think I was useful to them. I went to work at a *chai* stall, but after a few days the tea seller sacked me. Then I worked for a *chaat pakodi* vendor for a few weeks but then he stopped using his cart. After that I worked for 3 or 4 months at a non-vegetarian *dhaba*. I washed dishes and caried plates from 8 a.m. until 11 at night. The owner used to give Aunty thirty rupees a day for my work. The cooking pans were very big and heavy. It was a real struggle for me to wash them, but I had a compulsion to prove that I could do it well.

The worst part was that I had to wash the pans and plates behind the building at a tap right next to the toilet. It wasn't there for the customers, it was for the owner and the workers to use. If the customers had seen it, they would have never returned. It was the dirtiest, smelliest toilet in the world. It never got cleaned and it didn't have a door, just a blanket stretched across the entrance. And, what was just as bad, I had to scrape all the food that was left on plates into a big plastic bucket next to the toilet. It wasn't emptied every day, it just sat there in the heat, so there were always flies around. Sometimes the smell from that toilet plus the big bucket of slop nearly made me throw up.

When I worked at the *dhaba*, I was always tired. I worked long days and I got very little sleep. But Aunty was always saying the same thing over and over: "If you want to stay here you have to work. Where do you think we'll get the money from to look after you both?" My sister was still doing all her housework. Also Aunty would never give me any food in the evening because she knew they used to give me things to eat at the *dhaba*. Sometimes they gave me food twice a day. They used to give me egg curry or *dal tandoor-roti* to eat. But sometimes the owner forgot. When he forgot, I never dared to ask, and so I just stayed hungry.

◆ ◆ ◆

The gambling was still going badly for Aunty. She didn't realise that she was to blame for her own money problems. She didn't think that stopping gambling might be the answer. There had to be another reason. So she consulted a tantric astrologer to find a solution. The tantric told her, "Your debts are very high, so there is only one solution left. You must go back to that colony where you lived before. Here you will never be able to succeed." Perhaps the neighbours had told him about all the noise at night and asked him to get rid of her. In any case, Aunty did what the tantric told her to do. Less than half a year after vacating the house, she took us back to that same colony. For me it was an improvement again. No more days crouched next to that smelly toilet washing pans.

Of course, we couldn't go back to the old house, but she rented a room nearby. Her reputation in the colony was so bad, I wonder why anybody would have rented her a room. But somebody did.

Soon after returning, her luck changed and things started to get better. Their debts were decreasing, they started to win more at cards, and Aunty thought that the tantric had been correct.

Then I was sent to work for a man who sold shoes and sandals from a handcart. He used to give Aunty twenty-five rupees a day for my work. I used to go with him at 10 a.m. and I returned around 6 or 7 in the evening. My job was to walk alongside the shoe hawker and shout, "Buy your shoes and sandals here." When he would take a nap after eating at lunchtime, I had to watch over the handcart for him to make sure nobody stole anything.

Life was very hard for me in those days, but I made some good friends. When I used to come back from working with the shoe hawker, I would have a little time in the evenings to play with them. Two of them became my best friends, and they still are. One is called Guddu. He's younger than me. And the other is also called Naresh. He's about my age.

I used to go to Guddu's house often to play. His mother used to ask him to bring me home. His family were lovely people. They were happy. And they were also *Sindhi*, like my family, so I could speak my best language with them. Now that he's an adult, Guddu doesn't like to speak the *Sindhi* language anymore, so we always speak *Hindi* when we meet.

Guddu's mother was really kind. She always asked if I was hungry. She used to give me whatever she was cooking for the family. When she was cooking something new, she always wanted me to try it, because she knew I loved good food. And sometimes she used to give me clothes to wear that she said her relatives' children had grown out of. Some of those clothes seemed new to me at the time. Looking back, I think she used to buy them for me. My own clothes were always worn out. Aunty used to say there was no money to buy clothes. So I would wear one tee shirt until it fell apart.

Guddu's father was also very kind. He had a fruit juice shop just inside the main Jaipur bus station at Sindhi Camp. One day Guddu's father asked me, "Would you like to come and work at my shop instead of working for the shoe seller? I'll give you better money – fifty rupees a day – plus I'll also give you plenty of fruit juice and food. All you will have to do is collect and wash the glasses." I really wanted to do it, so he talked to Aunty, and she agreed. My salary would be higher than with the shoe hawker, so she didn't mind.

Guddu's father started taking me to his shop early in the morning. When we arrived each day he would first give me breakfast and two glasses of fruit juice. On the first day he told me, "You only have to wash the glasses. And I want you to be comfortable doing it. There's no hurry. This is *our* shop. I want you to consider it to be your shop as well." It was the first time I had had a job that I liked. There was no stress. Nobody shouted at me if I did something wrong. Guddu's father treated me like his own son, and he paid my salary directly to me.

After work, he would drop me off outside Aunty's house on his way home, and Aunty would always be waiting there to immediately take the fifty rupees from me. But in the end, I only worked for about two weeks at his shop. Then the policemen at the bus station approached Guddu's father and told him that that getting children to do work was an offense. Of course it was illegal, but there were children working absolutely everywhere. Some people paid the police to look the other way. But Guddu's father wouldn't. So he told me, "I'm sorry son, but I can't let you work here anymore. Otherwise the police will make problems for me and I'll be fined."

It was a pity, but at least I was free again for a while. I knew it wouldn't last, but for a week I just stayed at the house and played with friends.

I had many friends in the neighbourhood, but they all used to go to school during the daytime. I wanted to go to school with them. Many times I would say to Aunty, "Please get me enrolled in school. I want to go and study like all of my friends do." But Aunty used to say, "No, you're too old to start school now. All the other kids of your age can already read. No school will take you. Anyway, you don't even have an ID card, so it's not possible." The last part, at least, was true. I had no birth certificate or ID card.

And without one, most schools wouldn't let me in. Aunty used to say, "You're too grown-up now for school. You need to earn your keep. How else can we afford to keep you and your sister? If you both want to eat, you need to bring in some money."

At that point, I believed that my life would never be about reading and writing and playing, like the other kids. My life would just be about working to earn money for Aunty and her son. We were nothing more to them than slaves. My sister did all their housework, and I was rented-out to earn money for them. All we got in return was a place on the floor to sleep. There seemed to be no way out and I felt like that's how my life would always be.

Not long after that, they put me to work again at a different juice shop. This one was outside the High Court at Collectorate Circle. There were always lots of police and lawyers around, but nobody objected to seeing a little kid working illegally at a juice shop this time. The shop owner was a friend of my so-called cousin. I earned just twenty rupees a day, which he paid directly to my cousin. In case you don't know, that's about 25 US cents. Again, my job was mainly to wash the glasses and keep the equipment clean.

I had to walk to work in the morning, and since it was about 4 or 5 km from the house I needed to leave very early. As soon as I arrived, I had to wash the juicer machine, and then start washing glasses. I would be busy until about 10 or 10:30 at night. Then I had to walk back to the house. So it was about 11 or 11:30 by the time I was back at Aunty's home. The days were long and hot, and I was always tired.

It wasn't too bad, but then I made a big mistake. One day the juice seller ran out of sugar. He borrowed a bike from a nearby shop and told me to cycle quickly to the store and buy a bag. He handed me fifty rupees to pay for it. But at the shop, when I reached into the pocket of my shorts, the money was gone. It must have fallen out on the way while I was pedalling.

I became very scared and started crying. It was the first

time he had trusted me with money, and I just couldn't believe I had lost it. I searched everywhere. I went back by the same route, looking the whole time to see if it was somewhere in the road. But somebody must have found it by then. I was really in a panic because I knew this would cause big problems.

There was nothing I could do but go back and tell the juice seller. Of course he was angry, but it wasn't his money, so he called the shop owner and told him that the boy had dropped his fifty rupees somewhere. The owner said the money would be taken from my salary. So I would have to work two-and-a-half days for free.

The owner must have told my cousin, because Aunty knew what had happened. When I got back that night, Aunty started beating me with a broom handle. While she was hitting me she was shouting, "Can't you do anything properly? You stupid boy. Do you know what I can buy with fifty rupees? Five kilos of flour! Vegetables! If you're careless then you don't eat, so you can go to bed with an empty stomach." I pleaded with her. I said, "Aunty, nothing like this will happen again. I'll work carefully. It was just an accident. The money must have fallen out of my pocket and blown away."

I wanted to leave, but I had no options. Where would I go? Who I would go to? I didn't even know the addresses of my real relatives. But I suppose I knew that I wasn't going to stay there much longer.

◆ ◆ ◆

The biggest problem working at that juice shop was that it was located in Bani Park. That's a fancy part of town where rich people live in big houses. There were no derelict buildings or wasteland around. If you've never lived on the street you won't understand this problem. Where do you take a crap when you need to go?

In Bani Park there was a public toilet, but that cost either

2 or 3 rupees, depending on what you needed to do. It was really not expensive. In America that would be about 3 cents. But I never had any money at all. Aunty took everything off me. Sometimes at work it made me very uncomfortable because I felt a lot of pressure inside. My natural time to go is early afternoon. But I had to keep it in all day until I got back to Aunty's home late at night.

Many times in the morning I would ask Aunty or her daughter-in-law for 3 rupees. I told them that if I eat something at lunch time, I feel a lot of pressure, and I need to visit the toilet. Just 2 rupees would be enough. At the public toilet, I could pretend I had only had a pee. But they always refused to give me any money. Sometimes, if it got really urgent, I used to ask the juice seller if he could give me an advance of 2 rupees. He used to say "No. The owner will refuse. He'll quarrel with me if I give you money." I used to tell him, "It's really serious. I need to go right now. If I speak to my cousin about it in the evening, he'll speak with the owner and have my salary reduced by 2 rupees."

It depended on his mood. Sometimes he would advance me the money, but usually he used to refuse. Perhaps he thought I was just pretending.

Then one day I had a problem with my stomach. It's not surprising. For lunch I used to take a tiffin tin with leftover food from Aunty's home. Sometimes it was vegetables that had been cooked two days earlier and left out for flies to walk on. I told the juice seller I needed to go urgently. But he refused to give me the 2 rupees I needed. I worked on for a while, but I started feeling hot and dizzy. And then I couldn't control it any longer.

I wonder if you can you imagine how it makes you feel when you shit yourself in the street in front of people. I was just a little kid, wearing shorts. There was no way I could hide it. I felt so ashamed. So I ran to the public toilet and went in under the pretext of washing my hands. It was free there if you only wanted to wash your hands. The attendant kept a close eye on people, but I sneaked inside to clean myself and wash my pants.

I tried to walk out silently, but my shorts were completely wet and the toilet attendant was not stupid. "What have you done in there?" he asked me. I lied and said, "Nothing. I just washed my hands." I knew he could tell though.

Then I felt very uncomfortable. I had tried to clean my shorts without any soap, and I had to wear them for the rest of the day in the summer heat. I knew that I smelt terrible and I tried my best to stay away from people.

I was terrified that it might happen again, and so I started thinking about a plan in case there was another emergency.

At the juice shop we had lots of regular customers. Some people came every day for a glass of papaya juice, or an orange and banana smoothie. Some were friendly. Others never spoke to me at all. One regular customer was called Satpal. He was a bodyguard for the judges at the High Court. I had seen him in the grounds of the court wearing a military uniform and carrying a machine gun. He looked pretty scary then, like a very serious soldier. But when he came to the juice shop he always wore normal clothes. He used to come most evenings to drink juice. Sometimes he would also come during the day, but in the evenings he would often sit for a long time.

Satpal always spoke to me, and sometimes if we were not busy, I would sit with him a while. He was a really kind man who never treated me like I was beneath him. He felt like a friend and I was always happy when he called to the shop.

The day after my accident, Satpal came in the evening when we were not busy. I was still very upset about it. He asked me what was wrong. He said he could see that I was bothered about something. I trusted him and so I told him what had happened. I explained that in the morning, as soon as I was awake, Aunty would give me some food for my tiffin tin and immediately after washing my face she would make me leave the house to walk to work. Often I didn't have time to wash at all, and there was almost never a chance to use the toilet. We shared a bathroom with three other families in the building, so there was always a queue there in the morning. And I told him that sometimes the juice seller wouldn't lend me two rupees when I needed to go. So I had made a mess of myself yesterday in front of all the customers because I had a stomach problem.

There are lots of good people in the world. When you need help, sometimes you meet one of them. From then on, a couple of times a week, Satpal would give me five or ten rupees tip for bringing his papaya juice. The tip was more than he paid for the drink. I would keep the money for the future, hidden away from Aunty. That took some of the stress away. Then somebody told me that there was medicine that you could take to stop you needing to go if your stomach was upset. So with some of the money from Satpal's tips, I bought two of those pills from the pharmacy. I wrapped them in silver foil and kept them in my pocket at all times, for emergencies. That took more of the stress away.

Then another solution appeared. Often I was asked to take fruit juice in to the offices of lawyers in the High Court building. The security guards all knew I was the juice kid, and they never stopped me going inside if I was carrying drinks. One day I realised that there was a toilet in the public area of the law courts that was free for anybody, even the little kid who delivers juice. If you were inside, you could use it. There was no attendant, and it didn't matter who you were. From then, after I had made my deliveries, I used to stop off there. They also had nice soap that smelled like roses. So I would always go back to work feeling fresh and clean.

◆ ◆ ◆

I suppose it was becoming clear to me that I had to solve the problem at Aunty's house too.

One day during the summer, I returned to Aunty's home at about 11:30 at night. I was tired and hungry. I hadn't eaten since lunchtime. But Aunty was gambling with my cousin and his wife, plus three of four other people. They were making a lot of noise and drinking alcohol. Aunty was too busy losing money to give me any food. When I finally got to eat, it was about 2 a.m., but the gambling continued for a couple more hours. Since my sister Raji and I used to sleep on the floor of the living room, it was maybe 5 a.m. before everyone had gone and we could lie down. I was so tired, I overslept and I was woken up at 7:30. So I was late for work, because I usually got up at 7.

The whole day I was feeling tired and slow. At one point, the juice seller asked, "What's the matter with you? You're really lethargic today. Didn't you sleep last night?" So I told him I didn't get much sleep. He knew that Aunty used to gamble. And he knew about my cousin too, that he was a lazy man who wanted to earn money from gambling instead of working. Then when I was sitting down during the afternoon when we had no customers, I fell asleep. The juice seller woke me up and said, "Tell me what's the matter. Why didn't you sleep last night?"

Sometimes he acted like a friend. But I knew he really just wanted information he could use. I made him swear that he wouldn't tell anyone. Especially the shop owner, who was a friend of my cousin. And then I told him all about the gambling and drinking and noise. I told him I didn't sleep the night before because Aunty had been gambling until even later than usual.

Of course I shouldn't have trusted him. At closing time, when the juice shop owner came to count his profits and bring supplies for the next day, he was told everything I had said. And later, when I arrived back at Aunty's house, the juice shop owner was just leaving. He had gone to a lot of trouble to tell tales on a little kid. He stood and looked at me in the street, then he kick-started his scooter and rode away.

Obviously there was going to be big trouble now. Aunty had been doing the washing that day, and she followed me inside holding the wooden paddle that she used to beat the wet clothes. She said, "What have you been telling everybody at the juice shop?" I knew there was no point saying anything, so I stayed silent. She said, "You told them we are always gambling and drinking. That we don't let you sleep. Gossiping about us." And she started hitting me with the clothes paddle. Every time I tried to move either Aunty or her daughter-in-law hit me with the wooden bat. Eventually I was all bruised and swollen.

The next morning Aunty was still angry. She roughly woke me up and said, "Wash your face, grab this food, and go to work." She slammed my tiffin tin down on the floor next to me. But I knew it was the end. I had lain awake most of the night curled up on the floor, thinking about what I should do. Turning it over and over in my head. I had decided I didn't care where I lived. I'd live anywhere, sleep anywhere, but I would not be living at Aunty's house from now on. It was especially difficult, because my sister also lived there, although they treated her much better than they treated me. I was just a money-making slave to them. My sister was obedient. She worked in the house and didn't cause them any problems.

I knew I would rather be homeless than live in fear at Aunty's home. And I was never going back to work for the traitor at the juice shop. I had decided to be calm about it and leave silently, without a word. Just never come back. But when I was outside the house something in my head snapped. I started to shout terrible, abusive things in the street about Aunty. I'm ashamed of what I said, but it was all true. Some of the neighbours came out to watch. When Aunty came outside I threw stones at the house so she had to go back indoors. I shouted about how she was a drunk and a gambler and much worse. There are other things about Aunty that I haven't told you. I shouted that I would be happy if I never saw her again in my whole life, and that I was never, ever, coming back.

Chapter 2: Becoming a slave

After I had escaped from Aunty's house, I wandered here and there all day in the Pink City. I had no idea what to do or where to go, so I just walked. I thought maybe I would see my papa somewhere by chance. So I looked carefully every time I saw a cycle-rickshaw. It was impossible. There were thousands of them on the streets of Jaipur.

I was feeling very nervous, but at least I was free. Nobody was going to hit me now for telling the truth.

Although I was just a small boy, I knew how dangerous the city could be at night. And I was really scared of street dogs after being bitten twice by Yellow Dog. After dark, when the streets are empty, packs of dogs roamed around looking for food, barking and howling, and fighting with each other. You really didn't want to be out on your own. And I understood that some people could be even more dangerous than street dogs. Also, I was hungry. I hadn't eaten anything the whole day long, because I had no money to buy food.

At the end of the day, I walked to the *Jhulelal* temple. All the *Sindhis* living in Jaipur went there sometimes. Most Indians have never heard of him, but *Jhulelal* is one of the main gods of the *Sindhi* people. *Ganesh*, with his elephant's head, is my own favourite god. Ganesh is a normal Hindu god. He helps you solve problems. But *Jhulelal* looks very different. He's an old man with a bushy white beard, sitting on a lotus flower on the back of a big fish. I had been to the temple a few times, and I knew there was a small, quiet park, just behind it, with some benches. I was planning to sleep there. I'm a *Sindhi*, I thought, perhaps *Jhulelal* will protect me.

When it was getting dark, I was sitting there on a bench in

the park, feeling very lonely and afraid. Sometimes it feels like the universe listens to you when you ask it for help. That day, the universe listened to me. I had no idea where my papa was, but during the afternoon he had called at Aunty's house to see his kids for the first time in months. My sister told him the whole story, about all the gambling and drinking, how badly Aunty treated us, and how she had beat me all night with the washing paddle. So my papa had spent the rest of the day cycling around the city trying to find me. Just as it was getting dark he looked over the wall of the *Jhulelal* Park and he saw me sitting on one of the concrete benches there. I was so happy to see him that I started crying.

Papa tried to persuade me to go back to Aunty's home. He said, "Where will you stay now? I sleep on the pavement. I cycle the rickshaw all day, so I can't keep you with me." Then he tried the same old story. He said, "Just go back for a short time. Give me one or two more months, then I'll have saved some money. I'll find a room and I'll take both you and your sister back." But I had heard that promise too many times before. I refused. I said, "No. I'll sleep anywhere. In the street. Wherever you sleep. But I will never go back to that witch's house. When I left, I made a promise to myself that I would never go back, no matter what happens."

Papa tried very hard to convince me. But he knew it was useless. Even when I was a little kid I could be very stubborn when I decided something. So he put me in his rickshaw and we went to buy some food. And of course papa also bought liquor for himself as well. Then we went to the military area of the city to sleep. Papa slept in the rickshaw and I slept down on the floor next to it. But Papa laid out his shawl for me, and I slept on that. That's how my life on the streets began.

The next morning, after we had drunk *chai*, papa put me on the *fanta* – that's the wooden luggage shelf at the back of a rickshaw – and we began cycling around in search of a customer. Sometimes if there was a family, the little kids would sit on the *fanta,* and their parents would sit on the seat. After a couple of hours we still hadn't found a customer, so we stopped near the bus stand to take a break. I sat on the rickshaw seat, but papa said, "If you're sitting in the rickshaw, how will I get a customer? People will think you're my passenger." So he told me to stand away at a distance, and when he had a customer, I could sit back on the *fanta*. He was right. Very soon he had a passenger. When I sat down, the customer asked, "Who is this? Why is he coming with us?" Papa said "He's my son. As you can see he doesn't have any shoes, so I'm going to take him to buy some when I have dropped you off. Then I'll take him home." The passenger said it was OK. Papa used that story each time a customer asked, or he would say he was taking me to buy some new clothes.

Some customers didn't bother to ask who I was. Others were afraid because I was sitting behind them where they couldn't see what I was doing. They thought I must be a pickpocket because my clothes were worn and dirty. There are people who believe they can see how honest you are by looking at your clothes. But I have met many dishonest people with beautiful clothes.

Life in the street started to become normal for me. We never stayed in the same place for long. At night we would always find a different place to park the rickshaw and sleep. Somewhere under a tree if possible, because if you were parked next to a tree in a dark street there was less chance of getting hit by a car.

Most nights papa used to drink far too much alcohol. He always became like a different person when he drank a lot. If he drank a little, it would make him sleepy, but when he drank a lot he changed. Usually he was quiet and friendly to people. But after he drank liquor, he would become loud and shout a lot. He wouldn't sleep and used to quarrel for no reason with other street people. Sometimes they would start to fight. I used to get in between them and plead with him to stop. Usually, when people saw that he had a little kid with him they would walk away without fighting.

◆ ◆ ◆

Most rickshaw passengers are picked up when you are roaming around. They hail you from the side of the road. They don't usually come to you if you are stopped somewhere unless you are near a bus stand or a train station. And most of them don't like it if there is a little kid sitting on the luggage shelf. Sometimes if papa saw somebody trying to stop a rickshaw in the street he would tell me to get off. Then I would sit at the side of the road and wait until he dropped off his customer and came back to get me.

I knew that I made things more difficult for papa. So I thought I would try to make myself useful. Some roads in Jaipur are pretty steep. And some passengers are really heavy. If papa needed to cycle uphill and started to struggle with a heavy passenger and me sitting on the *fanta*, I would jump off and push the rickshaw from behind. One day when I was pushing the rickshaw, I got too close to the axel. The bicycle chain goes around a cog on the back axel, and it's not covered. My shorts were far too big for me and they got caught in the cycle chain. I was a skinny little kid and I weighed nothing, so I got pulled under the rickshaw. My shorts got ripped and my foot was bleeding. Although I made a lot of noise, it wasn't as serious as it sounded and I wasn't really hurt.

The passenger started to panic. He got off the rickshaw and paid quickly. Then he ran away. He didn't even wait for his change. He was probably worried that the police might get involved and he would have to give a statement.

Papa was very angry with me. He took me to a small clinic to get bandaged and he gave me his spare pants to wear. They were also far too big for me and the legs had to be rolled up half way. He told me I must never do that again. He said if he was going uphill, he would get off and push the rickshaw, I had to stay sitting down. I still have a scar on my foot from that accident.

◆ ◆ ◆

We got into a daily routine. When we woke up in the morning, we would go to the public toilet – if papa had enough money over from the day before – to take a crap and wash our hands and faces. If there was no money, we would take bottles of water and go take a crap in a derelict house, or down by the railway line. Like I told you, it can be a real problem for street people. Then we would drink *chai* and eat breakfast if there was enough money over. Otherwise we would roam around to find a passenger to get money so we could eat something.

About once a month, if papa had a little money to spare, we would buy some old second-hand clothes from a hawker. Each Sunday there was a market near the Sanganeri gate. That's the main place to enter to the Pink City. Hawkers used to take barrows there piled high with old clothes. Everything was mixed up so you would need to spend a lot of time to find something good that fitted you. Then we would buy some pants and a shirt to wear for the next month until they wore out. It was normal for me to wear the same clothes for two weeks or longer. We used to take a shower only a couple of times a month in the public bathhouse because it was so expensive. Then we would take our spare clothes to wash at the same time, and later we would let them dry on the roof of the rickshaw in the sunshine. It used to cost eight rupees for one person plus some clothes. But if you took a lot of clothes they would charge another two rupees for each item. Getting clean and washing clothes would all take hours – the whole afternoon – so we would earn almost no money that day.

Sometimes, if things were going well with money, papa used to take me at night to see a movie at the Minerva cinema. Some people still called it by its old name, the Ganga Talkies. It used to be the cheapest cinema in Jaipur, but it's closed now. All the drug addicts and drunks and street people would go there. I loved it. Going to the cinema was the best thing that ever happened to me. At the Minerva they never had the latest films. They were more expensive to see, at one of the nice cinemas like the Raj Mandir. The films at the Minerva were always years out of date, or even old black-and-white films. Sometimes, during the show, the film would break, or the electricity would cut out. Then there would be lots of shouting and jeering until the film got started again. For three hours, I would sit there in a comfortable seat, in a magical Bollywood world, and I could forget about my own world. I used to love seeing those old films with Sanjay Dutt or Suniel Shetty. I still love to see them now.

In the summer, when the weather was hot and dry, life was OK. We could sleep anywhere. But the winter and the rainy season were both very bad for us.

In the winter, Jaipur gets cold at night. It's near the desert, and nights can be very cold in the desert. We didn't have many blankets because we had nowhere to keep them. All of our things – all our clothes and blankets – had to fit into the box under the rickshaw passenger seat. There was nowhere else to keep anything.

If we slept in a shop doorway or on a *verandah* – that's a covered pavement that they have outside some old-fashioned shops – the police would sometimes wake us up. They would always ask my papa, "Who is this?" And then they used to ask the same questions to me, "Who is this? Why are you sleeping here?" Sometimes, if we told the police we had nowhere to live, they would leave us alone. Other times they made us move on to sleep somewhere else, in some other shop doorway or *verandah*.

One night, when we were getting ready to sleep at the side of the road near to Sindhi Camp bus station, a man stopped to talk to us. He was friendly and he sat with us a while. It seemed strange to me, because nobody ever did that. But he had a reason. He must have come back later when he knew we were asleep. The next morning when we woke up, our flip-flops had been stolen and papa's money was gone. Papa used to keep his money rolled up in the sleeve of his shirt. Somehow, the thief had rolled down his sleeve and taken it while he was asleep. Papa mustn't have drunk too much that night because he slept through it. He always stayed awake if he drank a lot.

When we realised what had happened, we both laughed at how stupid we had been to get robbed in our sleep. And we laughed at the big effort the thief had made. We had nothing worth stealing. Papa had only 20 rupees up his sleeve that night, which is about 25 US cents. And what would you do with some worn-out smelly old flip-flops? It meant we had no money to drink *chai* or visit the public toilet that morning. But we had woken up without any money before, so it wasn't that bad. Also, papa had to cycle the rickshaw in bare feet until he could find some more flip-flops. We never had the money to buy new ones. We used to collect discarded ones in the street. If papa saw one when he was working, he would stop and pick it up. Then he would try to find one for the other foot. So it would be normal for me to wear one red and one blue flip-flop, and they would always be different sizes and too big for me. Still, it was better than walking barefoot. When we were at the bus station, papa would go and look near to the shoe stall, because if people bought new flip-flops, they often put them on straight away and left the old ones behind in the street. Then, at least, we would have a matching pair, even if they were the wrong size. If they were damaged, we could get them repaired for just a few rupees.

The rainy season was the worst. If it was raining a lot we would get almost no passengers and then we earned no money to buy food. In the rain, people would take a three-wheeled autorickshaw – a tuktuk – instead, even though they were more expensive. There's a folding canopy over a rickshaw to stop the passengers from getting wet when it rains, but their legs still get wet. And if we had a passenger when it was raining, papa would get soaked to the skin cycling at the front, and I would get drenched sitting on the *fanta* at the back. When it rained at night, it was impossible for us to sleep. We used to roam around trying to find somewhere with a little shelter that was not already occupied by a street person. If papa had some spare money, we might go and watch late films at the Minerva cinema to get out of the rain for a few hours. But sometimes we would spend the whole night standing up in a shop doorway because there was nowhere dry to lie down. Or we would sit in the rickshaw under the canopy all night. But we could never sleep like that with heavy rain hammering on the roof. In the morning when the *chai* stalls opened, we would go and sit there under a canvas to drink *chai* and get a bit warm. Then our clothes would be wet for hours, or maybe we would just stay wet the whole day until it started raining again. Life was very uncomfortable in the rainy season.

◆ ◆ ◆

When I began living with him, papa started visiting my sister more often at Aunty's home. But I never used to go inside with him. I would wait at the end of the road. Raji would come outside to meet us. We would take her in the rickshaw to get fruit juice from somewhere. Then after we had talked for a while, we would drop her back at Aunty's house. Papa used to give her some money to give to Aunty for her expenses. I had left my few clothes behind at Aunty's house, but she refused to give them to papa. She said she had paid for them, so she would keep them. I don't know why. Clothes are useless without somebody to wear them. And really, the mother of my friend Guddu had given them all to me.

We knew that it was very difficult for Raji after I left. She would tell us how they made her work in the house like a slave from early morning until late at night. All she got in return was some food and a place on the floor to sleep. She would tell us, "Aunty and her daughter-in-law taunt me all the time. They're always saying things like, 'Your stupid brother ran away after shouting abuse at us. And yet still we pay your expenses. How do you expect us to take care of you without any money?'" It always made us feel very bad to hear how Aunty treated Raji. But what could papa do? He couldn't take her away from them. It's much worse for a girl to live on the streets. No matter how bad it was at Aunty's house, at least she had a roof over her head when it rained.

Papa thought it might be a good idea if Raji went to live with his sister – my *bua* – in Ajmer. He phoned her to ask. In those days you would have to go to a phone shop and pay to make a call. Only rich people had a mobile phone then, but my *bua* had one of the first pre-paid mobile phones, a TATA-Indicom. At the start, my *bua* said no. She said she couldn't afford to keep Raji. And of course she knew my papa wouldn't send her enough money. But then she changed her mind. It seemed that there were constant problems between her husband and my grandmother, who was still living with them. They had decided to send my grandmother to an *ashram* where old ladies who had no family to look after them could stay until they died. Of course, my grandmother did have family. But she was sick of arguing with her son-in-law, and she also wanted to leave. So a room was arranged for her in the old ladies' *ashram*. Since grandmother was too old and ill to look after herself, it was decided that Raji would go and live with her in the *ashram* to take care of her needs.

The next day, Raji was sent by bus to Ajmer and my *bua* met her at the bus station and took her to the *ashram*.

Life remained hard for Raji, but looking after grandmother was much better than being a slave in Aunty's house. I was pleased about that. From that day on, we never ever went back to Aunty's house.

◆ ◆ ◆

Working in a *chai* shop was almost a family tradition. My grandfather had had a *chai* stall, and so my papa had worked there when he was a kid, collecting glasses and serving customers.

One day a rickshaw driver had told papa that they needed a boy at a big *chai* stall near to the M.I. road. He said it would be a good way to get rid of me. I didn't want to work there, but I knew it was difficult for papa to earn enough with me always sitting on the *fanta* at the back of his rickshaw. So he went to ask about the job.

The *chai* boss was a very serious old man. He was disabled, so he use to sit the whole day high up in the *chai* stall where he could see everything, handling the money. He needed other people to do the work for him, otherwise he couldn't run his business. But he always wanted to watch what was going on. He also owned lots of cycle-rickshaws, which he rented out for fifteen rupees a day, and two taxis, which he rented out for a lot more. Most of his rickshaw *wallas* slept in the street, near to his *chai* stall. The police never bothered them. I guess the *chai* boss had an arrangement with them.

Papa spoke with him and I listened to them talking about me. The *chai* boss asked, "Has he ever worked before?" Papa said "Yes, he's worked before in a *chai* shop." Then he asked papa, "And where do you live?" Papa lied to him and said, "We live in a rented house quite far away. But I'll bring him to work early in the morning before I start working." They came to some arrangement about money, and it was agreed. From then on papa used to take me to work there at 8 or 9 a.m., and I worked until about 7:30 p.m.

For some weeks papa would drop me off every morning at the *chai* stall. The *chai* boss was a very rich man. He owned three or four properties in Jaipur, big houses that he rented out, but still every day he came to sell *chai* and count his money. He was also a very sad man, and at the start, I felt really sorry for him. I never once saw him smile. He had a very bad cough and no legs. When he was young he had been drunk and had had an accident. Somehow he had fallen onto a railway track and the bottom half of his legs had been chopped off by a train. They say he never drank alcohol again after that day.

His family was from Nepal. In India, Nepali people have the reputation for being very honest. They usually work as chefs, drivers, or bodyguards. They also have the reputation of being very good fighters. The *chai* boss thought he was really tough too, and he often argued with people, sometimes even with his own customers. He once had a big argument with three or four men, and I heard him shout at them, "I may have no legs, I'm still a man. If you make me come down there I'll beat the lot of you up. Don't think I'm weak just because I'm handicapped." But they all laughed at him and walked away.

If he was in a good mood, the *chai* boss used to give me two toasts to eat for breakfast. But if he was in a bad mood, as he usually was, he would forget, and he would only give me *chai* to drink. When that happened, if papa had earned some money, he would give me one or two rupees and I would have to buy a toast from the *chai* boss. He always took the money from me. It seemed like a pity for such a rich man to be worried about earning one rupee from a hungry little kid.

Then one day the *chai* boss said to me, "I come here every morning at 5 o'clock. Sometimes I'm even here at 4 o'clock. So I want a boy who can be here at 5 a.m. to help me open the shop and fetch water from the standpipe. But you live too far away. You arrive here at 8 or 9 in the morning. That's not good enough. If you can come here at 5 in the morning then you can continue to work for me. Otherwise, I'll have to find someone else."

I have never liked to get up early in the morning, but I needed to keep the job. So I told him I would speak with my papa later that day. Papa told him, "I lied to you when I said we lived in a rented room. We have no home. We sleep each night in a different place. Sometimes on the pavement, or near the railway station or in the military area. We have to move around because the police bother us if we stay in the same place. But if we could sleep here, next to the *chai* shop each night, in the morning when you arrive, Naresh will be here to help you." The *chai* boss said, "OK, you can sleep here. Most of my rickshaw drivers also sleep here. If any of them causes a problem, just mention my name and they won't bother you again." Then papa asked, "What about the police? Don't they make problems?" And he said, "No, the police don't come here. If the police come and trouble you then tell them my name and it will be OK."

So we made our home on the pavement in Mahavir Marg. We slept next to the wall that surrounds the grounds of the Jai Club, where all the richest people in Jaipur went at night to eat and drink alcohol. It was much better than always looking for somewhere new every night to avoid the police. That place, in the street near to the *chai* stall, would become my home – off and on – for years.

From then on, the *chai* boss would arrive each day at 5 a.m. and he would wake my papa. Then my papa would wake me, and I would have to start work immediately after washing my face at the standpipe in the road. Papa used to fetch water for the *chai*, because the water container was too heavy for me to carry.

It was busy there from very early in the morning. We had many customers as soon as the first *chai* was made. Everybody used to come there. Lots of street people, cycle-rickshaw *wallas*, balloon and trinket sellers, tuktuk drivers, and bus drivers. A bit later on, more people would stop in their cars after they had dropped their kids at school. Everyone used to drink their early morning *chai* there, except me. I was so busy that the *chai* boss never used to give me a drink until it was quiet, later in the morning. I was busy collecting and washing glasses, carrying cups of *chai* to customers, and passing out newspapers, tobacco, *beedis*, and cigarettes. Maybe you already know that *beedis* are little Indian cigars? They are made from tobacco rolled up in a *tendu* leaf and tied with string. They're much cheaper than cigarettes.

The *chai* boss always hated it if somebody had a special request. If somebody asked for *masala chai*, which is made with spices, he used to growl at them, "If you want that fancy *chai*, then go to the M.I. road to get it." Sometimes *Gujerati* people would ask for *kartewari chai*, which is very sweet. People who smoked *ghanja* in a *chillum* pipe also used to order *chai* with extra sugar in it. The *chai* boss didn't like that because it cost him more sugar.

I used to get scolded a lot by the *chai* boss, because, whatever my papa had told him, I had no experience at all working in a *chai* shop. I didn't know how to carry several glasses at the same time, and the *chai* boss didn't have those little wire racks that allow you to carry six at a time. All the *chai* stalls had them. I think he was too mean to buy one. So sometimes I used to get boiling *chai* on my hands, and the glasses used to be very hot. My hands were too small to carry four at time, so I could only manage two.

By 8 or 9 o'clock, most people would be at work, and the number of customers used to decrease a bit. Then I would finally have a chance to wash my face and go to the bathroom. After asking permission from the *chai* boss, I used to take a bottle of water to an old derelict house, a short walk away. There were no public washrooms nearby, and anyway, I didn't have any money. That old house was used by lots of rickshaw pullers, tuktuk drivers, and rough sleepers. Everyone used to go there to take a crap. It was huge and ramshackle, and the garden was overgrown like a jungle. No normal people would ever go there so it was pretty private. Then, after washing my hands, I would be back serving *chai* and *beedis* to customers.

At about midday we would get busy again. Then the labourers used to come to drink *chai*, and the office workers would come during their lunch breaks to buy *chai* and biscuits, or tobacco.

At around 2 or 2:30 in the afternoon, it would get quiet again. Then I would finally be completely free until 3 o'clock.

My papa used to bring me food from a *dhaba*. That was the best time of the day. I was always looking forward to what he might bring. Sometimes he used to bring delicious *aloo ka paratha* stuffed potato pancakes, or maybe *puri sabji,* which are puffed up flat breads served with potato curry. A special treat for me would be *mirchi ke tipore.* That's a typical Rajasthani dish of deep-fried green chillies that you eat with hot fresh chapattis. By then I was always really hungry. So we would sit and eat together.

At around 3:30 or 4 o'clock in the afternoon, another wave of customers would start arriving so I had to get back to work.

In the evening the *chai* boss would give me the big milk churns to wash, and also the metal cauldron that the *chai* was boiled in over a fire. That cauldron was completely burnt black because he never used to wash it even once during the day. It was too heavy for me to carry on my own, so I used to ask some of the rickshaw pullers to help. There were always some of them around who hired their rickshaw from the *chai* boss. Sometimes they even used to help me wash it, but sometimes they couldn't be bothered, especially if they had already started drinking alcohol. Then I used to struggle to wash it myself. I always did my best, but the *chai* boss used to get very angry. He would shout, "You don't even know how to wash something. It's still dirty. Go and wash it again. But do it properly this time."

So I would struggle with the big heavy cauldron once again. Or if papa was there, sometimes he used to wash it for me. Then, after he had locked away all the glasses and tools, and closed the shop, the *chai* boss used to get down from his seat and sit in his vehicle. He had a little three-wheeler motorcycle that he could control using only his hands. After starting the vehicle he used to give papa 20 rupees for my day of work. Then papa used to take me in his rickshaw for dinner. If he hadn't earned much during the day, we would first roam around for a while trying to find a customer. When we would go to eat, papa used to always buy a quart of liquor for himself, or sometimes more if he had enough money. So we would get back after having dinner by about midnight.

◆ ◆ ◆

I guess the *chai* boss wasn't such a bad guy underneath it all. He had a son called Veeru. The boy was actually the son of a Nepali tuktuk driver who couldn't afford to keep him. So the *chai* boss had adopted him to save him from living on the street. He never had a son of his own, but he had a daughter who was older than Veeru.

Each morning, around 8 a.m., Veeru would stop on his way to school in the back of a rickshaw and he would drop off food for his father. His school was just around the corner at the *Gujerati Samaj*. Then, at about 2:30 in the afternoon, he used to come straight to the *chai* stall after he got out of school. Veeru was a few years younger than me, but we had become good friends. It didn't matter to him that he was a rich boy who had nice clothes and went to school, and I was just his father's worker. We used to talk in the evening, if there was some free time for me.

Sometimes if there were no customers at the *chai* shop, we used to play together. But the *chai* boss didn't like that. One day he got very angry. He shouted, "Do I pay you to work or to play? If you have nothing to do sit quietly or find some work to do. I don't want you playing with my son anymore."

Veeru was also afraid of his father. So he came and sat near to me and he said, "If we can't play, then we can do one thing while sitting quietly. We can both count cars. Your time will pass, and my time will also pass." Time had no value to me then. I just wanted the day to pass as quickly as possible. So we did that most days. He used to count the cars passing on one side and I would count them on the other side. The next day we would switch over and he would count them coming from the left and I would count them from the right. It was our secret game, and the *chai* boss never knew we were playing it together.

Some years later, when the *chai* boss passed away, his family threw Veeru out onto the street. He was only about fourteen years of age at the time. They didn't want him to get any of the money or property because he was adopted, so they cut him off. I still see him sometimes around Jaipur. He's in his 20s now and works as a delivery boy, delivering food from restaurants on a scooter. It's an unusual job for somebody who grew up as a rich man's son.

◆ ◆ ◆

There was a big foreigner's restaurant across the road from the *chai* stall, behind a high wall. It was called the Indiana Restaurant. They say the owner used to live in Indiana, America, so he understood what foreigners wanted from a restaurant. And he thought the name was clever, American and Indian at the same time, India-na. It was very expensive and it had a big garden where people could eat outside in the cool evening. That was quite unusual in Jaipur. They also used to have *Kalbelia* musicians and dancers to entertain the tourists while they ate. The *Kalbelia* are a tribe of desert gypsies. The men play music and some keep cobras and other snakes. The women wear long coloured dresses and they dance very well. The *Kalbelia* also worship the snake god, especially once a year on the snake festival of *Naga Panchami*.

Those music performances only used to happen in the evening time. The restaurant would be open all day, from 10 a.m. onwards, but the foreigners would mainly come in the evening. Often coach-loads of foreigners would arrive who were on holiday travelling around India. The coaches would park nearby, waiting to take the tourists back to their hotels, and they would stay there until after midnight. Sometimes they would park right where we used to sleep. When street people have a regular place to sleep, it becomes their home. They *always* sleep there, and everybody understands that it's their spot and respects that. So then we would have to wait for the coaches to leave before we could lie down. It didn't leave much time to sleep, because I would be woken up to start work again at 5 a.m. That was my life. Always working and never enough sleep.

I didn't take a shower often when I worked at the *chai* stall. I never had the time or money to take a shower. Sometimes I only had the one set of clothes, so it was difficult to wash my clothes until I had got other ones to change into. So I would wear the same clothes without taking a shower for maybe three of four weeks. I would just wash my face in the morning.

On days when the *chai* stall stayed closed, like public holidays, or if the *chai* boss was sick, I used to go to the public bathhouse to take a shower and wash my clothes. It cost almost a day's salary for me, so I couldn't go often.

At the Indiana Restaurant, when the foreigners had eaten, they used to sit in their air-conditioned coach waiting for the others to arrive. Some of them would watch me working through the window. They would wave at me and say hello. And I would wave back at them.

I knew that they felt sorry for me. Sometimes they would get off the bus and give me chocolate or even a tee shirt that they had bought as a present to take home for their grandchildren. Once a foreigner came back the next day and gave me flip-flops that he had bought for me because I didn't have any shoes at the time. Often they would give me soap because I looked so dirty, with my long hair and tattered clothes. They used to use hand gestures to show me that I should use the soap to wash myself. I knew that they meant it kindly, but I knew how soap worked. I just didn't have the time or money to go to the bathhouse.

But sometimes, if I was lucky, a tourist would give me fifty or maybe even one hundred rupees. That always made me really happy, because I had to work five days to earn that much. Then I could go and take a shower, and we would have money to eat as well.

Chapter 3: The mean old executioner

The *chai* boss often used to send me to buy things for the shop when he was running low, like *beedis*, cigarettes, sugar, or tea. Of course I had to go on foot and sometimes it would take me an hour or more. Nothing I did was ever good enough for him. When I returned he would usually shout at me and tell me that time was money and I was too slow. I used to say, "Boss, it takes time. The shop is far away. I have to walk there, and it's always crowded. I have to wait to be served. I can't do it any quicker."

One day when I returned with some packs of tobacco he told me, as usual, that I was lazy and I had walked too slowly. But I had had an idea. The *chai* boss rented out cycle-rickshaws. He owned about 6 or 7 of them. Usually there was at least one sitting unused next to the *chai* stall. So I said to him, "Boss, if you let me learn how to ride that spare rickshaw, I could fetch your supplies really quickly and carry much more too."

"No, you're too small to drive a rickshaw," he said. "Perhaps when you're bigger, you can learn. Then you can cycle to the shops instead of wasting my time like this."

I thought it was a pretty good idea and I wasn't going to give up that easily. And I thought it might be fun, because I had always been fond of cycling. When I used to live at Aunty's house, most of my friends had bikes. They used to ride around the colony, and sometimes I used to ask if I could borrow one so I could cycle for a while. At that time I loved to cycle and I really wanted to have a bike of my own. But I had no money for anything at all. I could certainly never own my own bike. Although the *chai* boss had said no, I could tell I had planted an idea in his head.

Some evenings, after we had eaten dinner, we would get

back to our sleeping place near the *chai* stall earlier than usual so papa could sit somewhere and drink. He would usually sit alone so he didn't have to share his liquor with anybody. If he drank with other people he would always end up arguing about them taking more than they gave.

On those early evenings, when he had settled down with his bottles, I used to take his rickshaw and drive it up and down the road. I was too small for my feet to reach the pedals so I used to ride it 'scissor style.' That's what we call it in India, the way that a little kid can ride a full-sized bike. You don't sit on the seat, you put one leg under the crossbar and crouch there with the crossbar under your armpit. Because your weight is over to one side, it's easy to fall. The rickshaw tipped over many times and sometimes I got hurt, but I was determined to learn. So each time I fell, I got right back up and tried again. And slowly, slowly I learned to drive a rickshaw scissor style.

From then, each time I was sent to fetch supplies I used to say, "Boss, let me borrow a rickshaw. I'll collect your things really quickly." He wouldn't hear of it. He was afraid, but not for me. He would say, "And what happens if you cause an accident with my rickshaw? Then the police will come knocking on my door."

Then one day he realised he had made a big mistake. He had forgotten to bring supplies with him that morning and the tea was completely finished. That's not good when your business is to sell tea. So he told me to take a rickshaw and fetch a pack of tea from the wholesale shop as quickly as possible. I jumped at the chance. I made sure I was back with his tea very quickly. From that point he always let me take a rickshaw to fetch his supplies.

I used to feel really happy when I was driving the rickshaw, when I was away from the *chai* stall cycling into town to buy supplies. So I started keeping an eye on the supplies. When things were running low, I would say, "Boss, you're nearly out of tobacco. Shall I go and fetch some?" You lose money if you run out of things to sell, so he usually agreed. And then he started to rely on me. He wouldn't bother to pick things up himself because he knew I would check his supplies and fetch things before they ran out. But I didn't really do it help him. I did it because I loved escaping from the *chai* stall and driving into the Pink City. I felt free then. The more I drove the rickshaw, the better I got at it.

◆ ◆ ◆

Then one day the chai boss got sick. They said he had a problem with one of his kidneys and he needed an operation. So, without any warning, he didn't come to open the *chai* stall in the morning for more than two weeks. I had nothing to do, so papa used to roam around with me sitting on the back of his rickshaw, just like before. I suppose he expected me to end up cycling a rickshaw for the rest of my life as well. So while we were looking for a customer, he would tell me where we where. He would say, "This is called Statue Circle. The railway station is down that way. Now we're in C-Scheme." None of the rickshaw pullers could read a map. None of them could read anything at all. They were all illiterate. So they needed to remember the names of everywhere.

We started going to the army area to eat in the evening because there was a great *dhaba* there. It was run by an old married couple, and they were really the best cooks in Jaipur. At that *dhaba*, you could get roti and vegetables for just a few rupees. For one rupee you could get a portion of *mirchi ke tipore*. And those stuffed, fried chilis were just the best rupee you ever spent in your whole life.

The food was so good that papa used to take me there most days. It was quite far, but with the *chai* boss away, we didn't need to be near the *chai* stall during the day. We did return each night to our spot next to the wall of the Jai club. Often, after we had eaten in the afternoon, we would sleep for a while near to the *dhaba*. There were nice houses there because some of the important military people lived there.

One day a woman came out the house we used to sleep in front of. She said to me, "Who are you?" And she pointed to my papa and said, "And who is he? Why are you with him?" So I said, "He's my father." She sounded angry, but I think she was just nervous speaking to us. She said, "Why are you sleeping here?" So I told her about working at the *chai* stall, and about the *chai* boss's kidney stone. And I told her we always slept there at the *chai* stall, but we just took a nap here after we had eaten in the afternoon.

She went back into her house and five minutes later she returned with a bag of food and fruit. She handed it to me and she said to my papa, "Why is your son so dirty? Why don't you keep him clean? He needs to throw those filthy clothes away. And why is his hair so long? He looks like a girl. Get his hair cut!" Papa didn't have an answer for her. He didn't know how to speak to rich people. So he just stood looking at her. Then she said to me, "Little boy, why are you so dirty? You even have dirt on your ears and neck. Why don't you take a bath? And why don't you change those filthy clothes?"

So I said, "Madam, I do take a shower sometimes. But it costs a lot of money to take a shower. And these are the only clothes I own. Even when I'm clean, I have to put them back on."

She went away again, and she returned carrying three pair of pants and a few shirts that belonged to her son. They were about my size. She said, "Please take these. Even if you can't take a shower, throw those clothes away and wear these instead."

I guess papa got the message. He said to the lady, "OK, later today I'll find a tap somewhere and I'll make sure he gets washed."

On our way back to the *chai* stall that evening, we stopped outside a hospital in Bani Park, where we knew there was a standpipe in the street. Papa washed me using soap and got all the dirt out of my ears and off my neck. Then he dressed me in the clothes the lady had given to me. He didn't get my hair cut, although it was long like a girl's hair. But I looked good after getting clean with my new clothes on. Papa had found a pair of flip-flops a couple of days earlier, so I put those on too, and I felt like I looked really cool.

◆ ◆ ◆

After a couple of weeks, the *chai* boss recovered and he was back, sitting high up in his stall, watching over everything and taking care of the money. He had been operated on at the hospital, and they had taken a stone out of his kidney. He didn't seem to be any happier though. So I was back at work, and we were back into our old daily routine.

It was winter time, which is wedding season in Rajasthan. Often, in the evenings, the rickshaw pullers who slept at the *chai* stall would go and work at a wedding garden. It was good money, but hard work. They would do catering work. Some worked at the *tandoor*, which is a big oven made of bricks and clay with a fire inside. Others cooked vegetables.

At about 5 o'clock, everyone used to go to do their second job, and they would come back at around 3 or 4 in the morning to sleep. If you worked in a wedding garden, you could take home any food that was left over at the end of the night, so they would all come back with plastic bags full of food for the next day. When they returned they would usually all eat together and drink alcohol. Somebody would light a fire of rubbish in the street and they would all sit around it. Everybody would be in high spirits and it was like a little party. They would give me lots of things to eat as well. The chapattis were always really good from the wedding garden. They contained lots of butter and they were cooked on the walls of the tandoor oven so they were smoky and crisp on the outside. Often they would share some *dal*, or *paneer* curry with me as well. All the rickshaw pullers became my friends. I was the only kid living among them so they all knew me.

One of them became my favourite. He was called Gafar. He

always kept his rickshaw decorated, and he had a radio in it, which was decorated with little lights. The rickshaw belonged to the *chai* boss and Gafar rented it, but he looked after it as if it was his own.

I used to admire his rickshaw. I used to think, when I grow up a little, I'll pull a rickshaw too, and I'll decorate it the way that Gafar does, with strings of coloured fairy lights. Every little kid is attracted to be something when they grow up. Maybe they want to be a cricket player, or a train driver, or a rich lawyer with a big car like their father. I was attracted to the rickshaw because there were only rickshaws around me and nothing else. That was my world. I only knew street people. The rickshaw pullers were my only friends.

Perhaps you don't know why they are called 'pullers' although they pedal cycle-rickshaws. Years ago, rickshaws were simpler. They had just two wheels like a market barrow, and the pullers would stand in between two handles at the front and pull them along, the way a bullock pulls a cart. You can imagine it. Big heavy rich people being pulled along by a skinny old man with no shoes on. That's not allowed anymore, but the lives of cycle-rickshaw pullers are not much better now.

The rickshaw pullers around the *chai* stall were always nice to me, but they all had their own way out at night. Some would smoke *ghanja* in a *chillam*, sitting around a fire of rubbish that they would collect together and light in the street. Others would drink *doda* tea made from dried poppies. Some would even inject drugs right into the veins of their arm. But most drank wine or strong liquor every night until they could hardly walk. It's not surprising really. Their lives were terrible, and they all knew that it would never get any better for them. There was no way out. They knew they would always sleep in the street. They would always get wet in the rainy season. They would never have money to do anything or go anywhere. Life would never be more than a fight to survive. Just a struggle to earn enough money to buy food. Most of them had no children to look after them, so they could never stop working no matter how old they were. That didn't really matter much because rickshaw pullers usually don't grow old anyway. Some of them look very old, but they aren't really. They have just had hard lives. So everyone had his own kind of intoxication, his own way to escape. I didn't imagine my life would ever be any better than theirs.

Sometimes if papa was late getting back at night I used to get scared. The rickshaw pullers would all be busy with their drink or drugs, sitting around their fires in the dark, and I would be left on my own. I was always worried that papa might leave me.

One evening papa was really late. He still wasn't back hours after the *chai* stall had closed. I sat for a long time on the corner of the main road, in front of the Indiana Restaurant, watching in the direction that papa usually came from. He'd never been so late before and I was so worried that I started crying. Then the manager of the restaurant came to me and asked, "What's the matter, why are you crying?" So I told him, "My father hasn't returned home. What will I do?" So he said, "Don't worry. He'll come. He's not going to leave you on your own. He must have had to take somebody a long way." He gave me a drink of water and made me sit nearby. He said, "You don't need to be afraid. Nothing will happen to you. I'll make sure of that." I was still sitting next to him when papa finally returned at about 11:30. Then the restaurant guy said to him, "You left your child alone at night and he was afraid. Why would you do that?" Papa told him that he was late because the rickshaw had got damaged and needed to be repaired.

When we went to our sleeping spot, papa was really annoyed. He said to me, "I was only late! Why were you afraid? I'm not going to leave you." But I was never really sure about that.

◆ ◆ ◆

Once again the *chai* boss didn't show up for a few days. They said he was having more problems with his kidneys. So we started going back to the military area to eat at the best *dhaba* in Jaipur.

There used to be an old train in that area on a track that wasn't used anymore. The train was a wreck, but it still had a toilet inside. The toilet only emptied onto the track below it, but when papa and I needed to go, we would always go to the train. I was a little kid and I thought it was quite fancy to sit in a train to take a crap instead of crouching in some bushes or a derelict house.

After eating, we would take a nap for few hours in the afternoon near the house where the lady had given me the clothes. I would always sleep on the ground and papa slept in the rickshaw.

One day when we woke up at about 4 o'clock, we went to drink some *chai*. Then I saw a foreigner trying to get a rickshaw in the street. I was always interested in foreigners, so I said to papa, "Let's ask the *ferengi* where he wants to go." Papa was afraid to speak to him. He said, "I can't speak any English. We won't understand him." But I gestured for the foreigner to sit in the rickshaw. I couldn't understand him, but I could hear he was saying: "... *Niro's Restaurant ... M.I. Road ...*" I knew the word 'restaurant,' and in Hindi, we also call it the M.I. Road, so I told papa we should take him. On the M.I. road we could ask somebody where Niro's Restaurant was.

The foreigner said, "How much?" Every rickshaw puller understands that much English. Papa showed him 5 fingers, but he shook his head and showed three fingers. So I showed him 4 fingers. But he smiled and said, "No. *Thirty five rupees, thirty five rupees ...*" He bent one of his fingers to show three-and-a-half. So I nodded and I sat down on the luggage rack at the back. But he made me sit on the seat next to him. He was trying to talk to me all the way in English, but I couldn't understand anything he said.

At the M.I. Road we asked some rickshaw pullers which one was Niro's Restaurant. It was all too easy, even without speaking any English. When we dropped him off, he handed me one hundred rupees instead of thirty five and he waved his hand to show me he didn't want change. That was almost a week's salary for me, and I was very happy, for about ten seconds. Standing outside the restaurant was the owner of papa's rickshaw. It seemed that papa hadn't paid the rickshaw rent for months. He hadn't mentioned that to me. The owner was very angry, and he said to papa, "Take the rickshaw to my house, park it and lock it there, and leave it. I don't trust you anymore. You never pay the rent, and I'm tired of searching for you."

Papa pleaded with him. He said, "I promise I'll pay the arrears little by little. Right now our situation is very bad. There's no work, and my boy is also homeless and we both sleep in the street. It's really difficult for us." But the rickshaw owner wouldn't listen. He said, "No. For months now you haven't paid anything. You're not using my rickshaw anymore. So take it to my house and leave it behind."

We had no choice. We cycled to his house and left the rickshaw behind. We had to walk back to the *chai* stall, but we still had the one hundred rupee note from the foreigner. So we ate something on the way, and papa bought himself a bottle of liquor to make him happy for the evening.

The next morning the *chai* boss was back. He'd already heard about papa's rickshaw. People talk. He could always see an opportunity to make some money, but he also knew about papa's reputation for not paying. So he said to me, "You talk to your papa. Ask if he wants to rent one of my rickshaws and I'll just deduct the rent each day from your salary." So it was agreed. I would work to pay the rent on papa's rickshaw. That's how it felt anyway. Since I only earned twenty rupees a day, and the rickshaw rent was fifteen, I used to work from 5 in the morning until the *chai* stall closed at 7 in the evening for just five rupees. That's less than 10 US cents.

It went on like this for weeks, but then one day my so-called cousin called by with some news from Ajmer. Aunty now had a telephone at home so she had been called. There was no other way to contact papa. My grandmother had passed away in the ashram. That meant papa needed to go to Ajmer for all the death rituals. He wanted me to go and stay with Aunty and my cousin again while he was away, but I refused. I told him I would sleep near to the *chai* stall where everybody knew me and I would be safe from the police. I was only eight or nine at the time, but papa already knew I could be very stubborn. There was no way he could make me go and stay with Aunty. He said he would send word to my cousin in about ten days, and then I should come to Ajmer for the final death rituals. He said I needed to work and save money to bring with me because he had almost nothing.

Since papa left me with his rickshaw, I decided to stop working at the *chai* stall for a few days, and use it to earn money to take to Ajmer. I didn't really have a choice. Rent would still have to be paid for it each day papa was away, and I couldn't save from just the five rupees a day that was left over. I couldn't even eat for that.

By then, as I told you, I had learned to ride scissor style, but I usually only fetched tea and sugar for the *chai* boss. I had only ever taken one customer. That was an old man who used to stop off sometimes for *chai* on his way to the Krishna temple in the Pink City. Occasionally I used to take him if nobody else was available. Everybody knew he always paid exactly 13 rupees for the trip. It took a lot of strength to pull the rickshaw with somebody sitting in it. He was a big, heavy man and I was very small for my age. That was the main problem. Because I was so small, no passengers wanted to go with me. I was lucky if I got one or two passengers a day. I used to roam around the streets for hours. I was desperate, so I would tell people over and over that they would be safe with me, that I would get them to their destination with no problems.

On a good day I used to earn only twenty or thirty rupees, occasionally a bit more. But some of that went on food. By the time papa sent word for me to come to Ajmer, with a lot of difficulty I had only managed to save seventy rupees. Less than one US dollar.

At that time, my so-called cousin was driving an autorickshaw. It obviously paid better than gambling. He said he would be driving Aunty to Ajmer for the final rituals and asked if I would like to go with them. There wasn't much choice, because the bus fare to Ajmer would already cost me fifty-five rupees.

Of course, I could have known what would happen. When we were already on the way, sitting in the back, Aunty said to me, "We're not taking you for free you know. You need to pay."

"I've only got seventy rupees in total," I told her. "I'll pay you later. Papa has no money. He needs it." But she said, "That's not my problem. Give the seventy rupees to my son to pay for his petrol."

When we reached grandmother's ashram in Ajmer, papa immediately asked me, "How much did you earn and how much did you save?" So I said, "I saved seventy rupees with great difficulty. But cousin snatched it off me to pay for the trip here."

Papa was angry. He said, "I expected to you bring me some cash. Your *bua* even had to pay for my head to be shaved because I have no money at all. I haven't smoked a single *beedi* for ten days, nor have I had a drink. You aren't a child anymore you know, you need to earn money." But it was starting to feel more like he was the child and I was the parent.

After a couple of days, all the death rituals were finally over. But what would happen now to Raji, my sister? With grandmother gone, she couldn't stay at the ashram any longer, and she really couldn't live on the streets in Jaipur as we did. So my *bua* agreed that Raji could stay with her for a while. Papa told her, "I'll send you money every month for her expenses." I suppose she knew her brother well enough to know that was not likely to happen. I decided I would have find a way to pay for Raji's keep myself.

We took the local train back to Jaipur. But the whole way I was very nervous about getting caught by the TTE – that's the ticket travel examiner – because we didn't have any money for tickets. The TTE can even call the police if they find you have no ticket. We couldn't take the bus back to Jaipur because you couldn't even get on a bus without a ticket.

The next morning, I started working at the *chai* stall again, and papa started driving his rickshaw. I had locked it outside Aunty's house while I was away.

Sometimes no matter how hard you try, there is always somebody who's angry with you. And usually it's about money somehow. Now the *chai* boss was angry with me. "Where did you go for so many days without informing me?" he asked. I told him, "My grandmother passed away, so papa went to Ajmer, and I was driving his rickshaw." Of course I should have told him beforehand, but I knew he would have stopped me.

He said, "Well then, you owe me two weeks' rent for my rickshaw." He knew papa wouldn't be able to pay it, and I had no money, so he said he would keep the five rupees he was paying me each day until the debt was paid off. That meant I would have to work for about six weeks with no pay at all, only to clear the debt.

Thankfully, there was a solution. It had turned to winter, and the marriage season had begun again. Perhaps you don't know this, but most weddings take place between January and March in Rajasthan. It's too hot to get married in the summer.

All the rickshaw drivers who used to sleep at the *chai* stall started to work at night in the marriage gardens. Sometimes if extra help was needed they used to take papa along. He didn't cook anything though, his job was to wash the plates and cooking pots. He used to earn 120 rupees for a night of work. He didn't go every night because sometimes he was too tired.

The rickshaw pullers arranged for me to work in the marriage garden after I had finished at the *chai* stall. I used to go and collect the dirty plates and glasses from around the garden, and help with the washing up. For that I'd earn seventy or eighty rupees a night. It was around 2 a.m. when papa and I would get back home. The washing up is the last job to be done, so it was always late when we were finished.

I used to often think of the time when I would go to the marriage gardens with my friends to eat and have fun, and now I was collecting the dirty cutlery and plates from under peoples' feet after I had worked all day at the *chai* stall.

I used to tell myself, "This is just a bad time in my life. One day it will pass, and the good days will come back. Then once again I'll be able to live a good life instead of only working all the time."

Sometimes I used to cry while I was working, but I had an urge to carry on. There was no choice. I needed to save money each month to pay for the keep of my sister in Ajmer, because papa didn't save anything ever. If he had some spare cash he would just spend it on liquor. Papa always took my salary from the *chai* stall, but I never gave the money I earned at the wedding garden to him. I used it to pay the arrears for papa's rickshaw, and then that was over I started to save.

When we visited Ajmer now and then, I would have saved a few hundred rupees for my sister's expenses. Money also needed to be saved for Raji's marriage. So I needed to keep working, no matter what.

None of the rickshaw pullers had a bank account. But there was an unofficial bank if they wanted to save money. The security guard at the Indiana Restaurant used to save money for the street people in his bank account. So I started giving him any spare money that I earned. It had to be a secret. I knew that if I told papa he would take it all and spend it on drink.

◆ ◆ ◆

One day, one of my papa's friends stayed with us for a few days at the *chai* stall. He was also a rickshaw puller, but he didn't have a rickshaw at the time and he had no money at all. He and papa used to get drunk together sometimes. That's what made them friends. Sometimes papa would give him money to buy *beedis* and used to pay for his food in the evening as well.

Papa suggested that when I had finished working, we should walk to a *dhaba* to eat instead of cycling there, and then his friend could borrow his rickshaw to earn some money during the night. But he would need to be back before 5 a.m. when the *chai* stall opened, because the *chai* boss would be angry if he found out and would want more rent for his rickshaw if he knew two people were using it.

That evening, his friend cycled off to find a customer while we went to eat. But the next morning, when the *chai* stall opened, he still hadn't returned.

The *chai* boss saw everything that was going on, and he quickly noticed the rickshaw was missing. You can imagine how he reacted when he heard what had happened. "I'm not interested in your excuses," he said to papa. "You'd better get my rickshaw back, or there'll be trouble." So papa borrowed a rickshaw and cycled all around Jaipur looking for his friend. But he was nowhere to be found.

Then papa had nothing to do all day. He used to hang around the *chai* stall while I was working. But of course most of my salary was still paying rent for the rickshaw, even though it had been stolen, so we had just five rupees left per day. In the evenings papa would try to get one of the other rickshaw pullers to lend him their rickshaw after they had finished working so he could earn some money during the night. The problem was that most of them slept in their rickshaw. Sometimes, one of them who always slept on the ground would lend it to him if papa promised to buy him some drink when he had earned a bit of money. But usually nobody would lend it. They were all friends, but they never really trusted each other.

Whenever papa had a borrowed rickshaw, he used to make me sit on the back and we would cycle all over Jaipur looking for a customer. My job was to watch out for the stolen rickshaw.

Papa's eyesight wasn't good at night. Like a lot of the rickshaw pullers and street people, he had poor eyesight, and it got worse as he got older. They say it comes from drinking bad liquor. When papa had almost no money to buy drink, sometimes we would go to a village just outside Jaipur where they made *kachchi daru*. In English you might call it moonshine. It was illegal, and the cheapest drink you could buy. It was also the most dangerous. The cheapest *kachchi daru* wasn't very strong, because it was only half finished. So to make it stronger, the sellers would add things. Everybody knew that. Sometimes they added chemicals, like cleaning fluid. Sometimes even *doda* from poppies. They say you need to eat chicken or mutton while you drink *kachchi daru,* otherwise it will make your muscles weak. They also say it can make you go blind or even kill you if you drink too much of it.

Night after night we searched for the stolen rickshaw. But eventually we had to admit that it was gone forever. Papa told this to the *chai* boss, and asked if he could rent another one. The *chai* boss had calmed down by then, but he wasn't a kind man. He was only interested in making a profit. He thought about it for a while, and then said, "OK, I'll rent you another rickshaw. But you'll have to pay the rent for *two* rickshaws. And because I don't trust you to pay thirty rupees a day, Naresh will work at the *chai* stall for free, and you'll pay ten rupees extra each day." That was about as good a solution as we could hope for. So once again I was working as a slave with no salary, just to pay-off papa's debts, and with no end in sight.

At the time, an old rickshaw like the stolen one was worth about three thousand rupees. Neither papa nor the *chai* boss talked directly about it. But it was simply understood that I would have to keep working at the *chai* stall for nothing until it was paid for.

◆ ◆ ◆

Sometimes you think this is the lowest point in your life. You think it can't get any worse. And then it does.

In the evenings, we used to lock the second rickshaw at the *chai* stall where it would be safe with so many people around, and we would walk to a muslim *dhaba* to eat. While we were walking, we would always keep a lookout for the stolen rickshaw. It became like an obsession. But really, it was a waste of effort. Papa's friend had probably taken it to another city and sold it by then. Or maybe he had taken it apart and sold the parts. We never saw him again.

One evening we were on our way home from the *dhaba*. We were talking and joking. Papa had only had a little bit to drink, so he was still in a good mood. And looking back he was already behaving a bit strangely. Then he seemed to trip over something in the street and he fell to the ground.

At first, I thought he had fallen on purpose to make me laugh. He could do funny things sometimes when he was in a good mood. But then he started screaming. He said he had badly hurt his back and he couldn't get up. Also his legs were hurting and they wouldn't work.

I took his key and ran to fetch his rickshaw. I lifted papa up and made him sit in it, and then I walked it back to the *chai* stall. He was still screaming all the way.

It was tourist season, so the Indiana Restaurant was really busy, and there were cars and tourist buses everywhere. Our spot was taken and there was nowhere for papa to lie down. I didn't know what to do. There was no room anywhere. But there was a metal box nearby where the *harijan* street cleaners used to keep their brooms and shovels. At that time street cleaning was a government job reserved for *harijan* women. It was supposed to help them because nobody would give them another job. The *harijan*'s box was about three feet high. Up to my chest at the time. I could see no alternative. So I put a blanket over the box and helped papa to lie on top of it. Every time he moved he started screaming again.

What on earth would I do now? The whole night papa was moaning and shouting about the pain. But he hadn't really fallen very hard. There was no blood anywhere, and no sign of any injury. I couldn't understand how it could be so serious. I started to think it was because he had drunk some bad *kachchi daru* with poison in it. Maybe he hadn't really hurt himself when he fell, maybe the bad liquor had poisoned his nerves and stopped his legs working, and that was why he fell in the first place. If so, he was lucky that he hadn't drunk very much of it.

In the morning, when the *chai* boss arrived, I told him what had happened and how papa had got hurt. For a moment he almost seemed concerned. He even gave papa a free cup of *chai*, and then asked him, "Is it ok now?" as if his *chai* was some kind of magic medicine. But papa said, "No, I can't stand up. My legs don't work and my whole body hurts."

I knew I needed to get him to a hospital, so I asked around the rickshaw pullers if one of them would help us and take him to a government hospital. But everybody had an excuse like, "I don't have time … I don't have any money … I need to go somewhere today." When you're in trouble, you learn who your real friends are, and papa suddenly seemed very short of real friends.

For three days papa stayed lying down on that box. He didn't get up once. When he wanted to pee, I had to give him a plastic bottle. Then, after three days, he needed to take a crap, and so helped him down and took him in the rickshaw to the derelict house nearby. He screamed every time he moved. When we got back he just lay down on the box again and stayed there. It was like he had decided to give up living. And near that box used to smell very bad because at night many people used to use the space behind it as a toilet, even when they could see my papa was sleeping there.

I had a little bit of money saved with the security guard at the Indiana, so I took it, and I promised one of the rickshaw pullers a bottle of wine that evening if he would take papa to the hospital.

The doctor couldn't tell what was wrong with him. He said, "He will need to have X-rays and tests done at a private clinic to find out what the problem is. And that will all cost a lot of money." I didn't have enough money saved to pay for any of that, so papa went back to lying on the metal box.

Everybody around us could see what was happening. Then somebody at the *chai* stall told me I should take him to see the *pahalwan*.

At the time I didn't know a *pahalwan* was, so I'm pretty sure you don't know. Only poor people in India who can't afford to see a proper doctor know about the *pahalwan*. In English the name means wrestler, but they aren't fighters, they're bone doctors. They can set broken bones or put your shoulder back if it gets dislocated. And they have special ayurvedic ointments for muscle problems. In the old days they used to work in the *akharas.* Those are wrestling gyms where people train and fight in competitions. There are still a couple of very old *akharas* left in the Pink City. In the old days, most of the *pahalwans* were Muslims, and they used to treat wrestlers who got hurt. Now they treat anybody who will pay them. They don't go to medical school, it's a family job. They learn how to treat bones and muscles from their fathers and grandfathers. And they are very cheap compared with hospitals.

I was told where I could find a good *pahalwan* in the Pink City, in the *Indira Bazar.* So I took papa there. The *pahalwan* was an old man, a Hindu, and he treated people in a small garden just off the road where all the statue makers have their workshops. Everything is always covered in white marble dust in that part of town.

According to the *pahalwan,* there were no problems with his bones or muscles. It was his nerves. He applied an ointment and a bandage and said, "Bring him back after four or five days." He also wrote down the names of medicines that I could buy at the pharmacy. But we had no money for them. After four days, I took papa back and got more ointment and bandages, but it didn't help, and by then all my savings were gone.

It was about that time that I started calling the *chai* boss 'the *jallaad*.' Not to his face though. In my head and under my breath. In English *jallaad* means 'executioner.' A *jallaad* pulls the lever in prison when somebody gets hanged.

I explained to him that I needed all my twenty rupees daily salary because papa couldn't work. We would settle any debts with him later, when times were better. At the time all of my salary went on the rental of the two rickshaws. He just said, "No." I pointed to papa's rickshaw chained up next to the *chai* stall. "Look, it's not being used," I told him. "You can rent it to somebody else if you want. Papa is sick. How can you expect us to pay rent for it?" So he said, "OK. I won't charge you for that one. But for the rickshaw that your father's friend stole from me, I'll still deduct fifteen rupees rent. So I'll give you five rupees a day, and not one paisa more."

I pleaded with him. I told him, "We can't eat on five rupees a day. Please take the money some other time. When papa is better you can take money for your rickshaw and deduct it from my salary if you want." But his final word on the matter was clear. "No. I don't know when your papa will get well. And it's not my problem. Somebody has got to pay the rent for my stolen rickshaw." He was a rich man, with big houses and other properties in Jaipur. He knew it was impossible for us both to live on less than ten US cents per day.

◆ ◆ ◆

For the first time in my life I was forced to beg. Each day I had to ask around the other rickshaw pullers if one of them would give me just one or two rupees. But I could never beg from strangers in the street. Only from people we knew. If I had a total of seven rupees, I knew I could buy some *tari* – I guess you would call that curry sauce or gravy – for four rupees, and three *chapattis* at one rupee each, from a very cheap Muslim *dhaba*. It was called the Sartaj Hotel. It's still there now, near to the Ajmeri Gate. It's nicer than it used to be, but it isn't anything like a hotel.

That's what we would share in the evenings, a plastic bag of *tari* and three *chapattis* from the Sartaj Hotel. Papa was unable even to sit up, so I had to feed him. During the daytime, because we had no money at all, we ate nothing. And the *jallaad* would sit there, perched like a mean old vulture, high up in his *chai* stall, counting his profits, and watching us slowly starve to death.

I hated begging, so at night after we had eaten our *tari* and *chapattis*, I would walk around the city trying to find empty beer and liquor bottles on the street. Some people would throw them away even though there was two rupees and fifty paisa deposit on a beer bottle and one rupee on a wine bottle. They couldn't be bothered to take them back to the shop. So I would take a plastic bag and I would collect them. They were often hidden behind tourist buses or cars. Lots of street people collected empties during the day, so I had to find the hidden ones that they missed in the evening. Sometimes I would find four or five bottles in an evening. The next morning I would sell them and then we could eat something during the day and I didn't need to beg for money to buy our *tari* and *chapattis*.

I started to keep a watch out. At night, cars used to come and park near the *chai* stall. I would see people drinking drink beer or liquor in their cars. Sometimes they would throw the bottle out of the car. Then I would grab it before somebody else saw it. But sometimes I'd watch them for hours, and they would drive way taking their empty bottles with them, and my efforts were wasted.

One regular customer used to come to the *chai* stall by bicycle at around three in the afternoon, several days a week. He was always neatly dressed. He wore glasses to read and he was very quiet. He used to drink only one *chai* and read a newspaper for a couple of hours, but he never really spoke with anybody. I never knew his name, but sometimes he would speak with me. When I had some bottle money, I used to ask if I could borrow his bike to go and buy food and *beedis* for papa during my afternoon break. There was no reason for a rich gentleman like him to trust his bike with some little street kid. But he always said yes.

When I cycled I was always very, very careful. But not because I was scared. Once, when I was in Ajmer and my sister still lived at the ashram with grandmother, I had some spare money so I rented a bike for two rupees. I'll tell you later how I had spare money. So I was cycling all around the city. Ajmer is not flat, some roads are quite steep. I was going down a hill really fast. It was fun, but I was going far too fast. Kids do things like that. Then two middle-aged ladies wearing traditional Rajasthani dresses stepped out into the street in front of me. That was when I realised the brakes didn't work very well. I swerved to try to miss them, but I hit one of them. She fell over and I fell off the bike. They both started screaming at me. I knew it was my fault. If the police come, I thought, they'll put me in one of those kid's prisons. I'd heard some very bad things about them. There were lots of stories around. Some other people started to shout at me and I panicked. I just left the rented bike behind and ran back to my *bua's* house. I never told anybody what had happened, and I stayed away from busy streets for days. I was afraid that the police would be out looking for me. I still feel really sorry that I hurt that lady. Since then I have always cycled carefully.

Sometimes I would borrow that same customer's bike to fetch a bag of millet for the *chai* boss. To gain some good *karma* in his life, the *chai* boss used to feed millet to the pigeons in the street. Well, he used to tell me to feed the millet to them. Often he would tell me to fetch a bag of it for him. I didn't want to ask him anymore if I could use one of his rickshaws to go, because he might have wanted rent for it then. So I would walk or borrow the customer's bike.

The old *jallaad* knew that three kilos of millet used to cost twenty four rupees in the Pink City. So he would give me exactly twenty four rupees to buy it with. That was almost what he paid me for five days of work at the time, just to feed to the birds. One day I asked around about the price of millet and I found another shop, a bit further away, that sold three kilos of millet for eighteen rupees.

I had never cheated the *chai* boss up to that point. But from then on, I always bought the cheaper millet for the pigeons and I kept the extra six rupees.

I knew it was wrong, and I felt guilty about it. Sometimes used to think I should give the six rupees back to him. But then what would happen if I didn't find enough bottles that day? Some days I only found one or two bottles. Then the birds would still eat, I told myself, but we wouldn't. And I remembered the many times I was pleading with the *jallaad* just pay me enough money for us to be able to buy food.

Eventually, he did start to pay me ten rupees a day. Just enough so that we didn't actually starve. Perhaps he knew that people had started talking behind his back about how mean he was being to us. But he was not happy about doing it. Sometimes, at the end of the day, he would get into his motor tricycle and I would stand there waiting to be paid before he went home. He liked to play the role of the powerful boss, like a gangster in a Bollywood film. So he would start up his vehicle and act as if he had forgotten about paying me, then throw my ten rupees onto the floor at my feet and drive away. That used to make me very angry. Then I used to think: no, why should I tell him the truth? Why should I give the six rupees to him? I have to go further to buy his millet for eighteen rupees. It takes my effort to get a cheaper price. When I was angry with him it felt easier to cheat him.

♦ ♦ ♦

The *chai* boss was still having problems with his health. Sometimes he would take a day or two off. He wouldn't tell anybody, he just didn't arrive in the morning. Then it would get very difficult for us.

Many times papa and I used to wait for him, and sometimes papa used to cry out, "What will we do now? When will my legs heal?" I used to tell him, "It will be fine soon. Don't worry, I'm here. I'll take care of you." But secretly I used to also worry about how we would eat that day and if papa would ever be able to walk again. Perhaps he would spend the rest of his life lying on that box in the street.

Now and then people would come in cars to distribute food to the street people. They would bring boxes of really nice vegetarian food. If we were lucky they would give us delicious hot *puris*, with potatoes, vegetables, and pickles. Sometimes we would even get *ladoos*, which are sweet balls made from chickpeas and flavoured with cardamom. After eating *tari* and *chapattis* every day for weeks, that all tasted so good. Then, for one day, our stomachs would be full and we would be happy. But otherwise I used to go walking around Jaipur in search of bottles to sell.

Then one time, the *chai* boss stayed away for more than two weeks. They said he was having pains in his kidneys again. After a few days I realised I just couldn't earn enough money from only empty bottles for us to survive. One day we had no money at all, and so we didn't eat anything all day. We just drank water. My papa was still very weak and I knew that if he didn't eat he would probably die in a couple of days. Then I became really scared that I might have to start begging money from strangers in the street, or do even worse things.

I could only think of one last option. Some of the *chai* boss's rickshaws were standing unrented, but they were all locked and he had the keys. I thought if I could use one, I could earn enough money for us to eat. So I walked to the *chai* boss's home. His house was about four or five kilometres from the *chai* stall, in Jyoti Nagar, close to the Rajasthan government building. He owned several big houses in Jaipur, which he rented out for a lot of money. Everybody knew that. But I was surprised to find he lived in a very small and simple place himself. It was a government house that he had lived in for many years. Those houses were very cheap to rent. Usually only poor people lived in places like that. He had probably been given it many years ago because he had no legs. It seemed like a strange place for such a rich man to live.

When he came to the door, I said to him, "Boss, we're really having a hard time because you haven't opened the *chai* stall. Papa still can't walk, he's just lying there. We've got no money at all. How we will survive?" So he said, "I'm sick! What do you expect me to do about it? And how did you get my home address?"

I told him, "All the rickshaw pullers know you live in Jyoti Nagar. I found your house by asking around the district which house you lived in."

He said, "How dare you come to my home! What do you want from me?"

I knew it was useless to ask for money, so I asked if I could borrow the key to one of his rickshaws so I could earn enough for us to eat while the *chai* stall stayed closed. Of course he got even more angry and he refused. He said, "And what if you break the rickshaw ... who will pay for the repair? What if the police arrest you? What will I say to them? What if this one gets stolen as well?" Then he became really abusive. He shouted some horrible things about me, and he told me to go away. I had worked for him for a long time and he knew those things he said about me were not true. I was really upset and also very angry with him. But usually I just felt really sorry for him. Because he was such a mean man, nobody liked him.

So how did we survive that period? There was a man who used to work at the Indiana Restaurant. His job was to keep everything working, like the generator and the fridges. He could fix anything. Everybody called him Pandit-ji. But that wasn't his real name. It just meant that he was very clever and everybody respected him. He lived in a room in the restaurant compound.

Pandit-ji used to see us both sleeping near the *chai* stall, and he saw me picking up bottles. I suppose he knew things had got really difficult for us. One night he asked me, "Have you eaten anything today?" I said, "Yes, I have," even though I hadn't. Then he said, "I work in the restaurant. Twice a day they make some simple food to feed the staff. I'll ask the cook to make a bit more than usual, so I can bring you some rice and *dal* each day." From then on, he used to bring us food that that been cooked in the kitchen of the fancy Indiana Restaurant. That was how we survived that period. Without the help of Pandit-ji, I don't know what I would have had to do.

Chapter 4: Getting rid of the lice

The rainy season was back again. Papa was still just lying all day on that metal box in the street. It was like he didn't even want to try to get better. He just lay there. Sometimes, when it got cold, I had to sleep next to him because we had only one blanket. I hated that. There was always a strong smell of urine around. People would come and take a pee behind the box as if they were unaware we were lying there. We were just street people, so there was no need to show us any respect.

But when the rains came, papa couldn't lie out in the open. I tried to get him to sit in a vacant rickshaw, but that was too painful for him. So I made him lie down on the *pyedhan*. That's the part of the rickshaw where people's feet go. We would both get soaked. Monsoon rain is very heavy.

There was a canvas covering part of the *chai* stall, but it was torn on both sides. When it rained, I could sit there at night with it covering my head, but water dripped everywhere. We couldn't sleep there and I couldn't take papa to find anywhere dry because his rickshaw was locked and the *chai* boss had the key. Sometimes I would spend the whole night standing under that canvas. I used to pray to God – to *Bhagwan*, as we say in Hindi – for the rain to stop so I could sleep for a while before starting work. Sometimes the rain didn't stop at all, and so we used to stay awake the whole night. Our blanket would be soaked as well as our clothes. I asked the *chai* boss many times, "Boss, can you please get the canvas repaired? It would be better for the customers when it rains." But I really wanted it fixed so we could sleep under it. He used to say, "Yes, yes, I'll get it changed." He never bothered to do it because it would have cost him some money.

By now months had passed without papa taking a shower or changing his clothes. I couldn't even remember the last time I had taken a shower myself. Our blanket was ripped and full of lice. It had got wet so many times that it had started to smell very bad. Eventually, one of the other rickshaw pullers gave us one of his blankets and so we threw the old one away. My clothes had also become itchy and uncomfortable. They were filthy and there were lice in them that used to bite me sometimes. One day, after the rain stopped, the sun came out. When I had a break from working at the *chai* stall, I took off my shirt and washed it. If you dry your clothes in the sunshine, the lice don't like it, and they run away. Sometimes that's the kind of thing you need to do in life. Let the sun shine on things to get rid of the lice.

◆ ◆ ◆

It felt like I had to make sure this was the lowest point in my life. I couldn't let things get any worse. But I knew that if things were ever going to change for the better, I would have to make a big effort to change them myself. Waiting around for something to happen was never going to work. I knew I needed to push papa to get well. For him to just lie forever on that box in the street simply wasn't good enough. And I decided that working twelve or fourteen hours a day to earn just enough money to eat *tari* and *chapattis* needed to end as well. The *chai* boss believed that he could do anything to us because papa owed him money. They had never even agreed how long I needed to work to pay off the debts. He thought he was so powerful that I would just work for him as his slave, forever. But I was starting to think differently.

◆ ◆ ◆

I told you that when I was in Ajmer one time I had enough spare cash to hire a bike, just for fun. Let me tell you about that time. It was not long after Raji was sent to live with our grandmother at the ashram in Ajmer, and before I started work at the *chai* stall. Papa and I went to Ajmer to visit Raji. At the time, papa still believed it was my fault that he didn't earn much money. He thought it was me sitting on the back of his rickshaw that stopped him getting customers. So just before we were to return to Jaipur, he locked me in a room at my *bua*'s house, and he went back alone. That made me feel very bad, like he didn't want to be with me anymore. After that I was always worried that he would leave me somewhere again. His big plan was to go back to Jaipur, where he could earn lots of money without me, and then come back to Ajmer in a few weeks when he had saved.

While I was stuck in Ajmer, I used to go out and walk around for hours each day looking for work. I tried everywhere in the market to get work, and I asked at many places, such as grocery stores, *chai* stalls, *pakoda* sellers, and *dhabas*, but no one hired me because I was very young, and nobody knew me in Ajmer.

Then one day I saw a kid, not much older than me, who was selling *kachoris* and *samosas* from a metal box on his shoulder. Maybe you know already what they are. They are little snacks. Indian street food. *Kachoris* are lentil fritters and *samosas* are fried pastry triangles full of spicy potatoes, onions, and vegetables. When you have tried a freshly cooked *kachori* or *samosa*, they are difficult to resist, because they are so tasty.

At that time there was big competition between the makers of *samosas* and *kachoris* in Ajmer. Everybody claimed his were the best. They all wanted to be the *kachori* king.

So I asked the kid who his employer was. He said nobody, he worked for himself. He picked up one hundred *kachoris* and *samosas* from a famous shop, and he sold them on the streets for one rupee each. He said, "When I have sold them, I give seventy rupees to the shop owner, and I keep thirty." That sounded pretty good to me. Not many little kids could earn thirty rupees in a day. So I asked him how long it took. He said sometimes up to six hours, but on a good day, just two or three hours.

He explained that if the shop owner didn't know you well, you needed to leave one hundred rupees deposit with him for the snacks, to stop you just running off with them. So it was decided.

That evening, I told my *bua* about my plan to sell snacks on the streets. I said I would need a box carry them in, and one hundred rupees deposit to start off. She had a box for me, but no money. But the next morning at the ashram, when I told Raji and my grandmother about it, my grandmother said, "It's good that you have found a way to earn money like that. You're clever, and a hard worker, just like your grandfather was. So I'll give you the money for your deposit."

When I arrived at the Gopi Samosa-Kachori Shop there were already a few boys waiting. I talked to the owner and he said he would let me sell his snacks. I paid the deposit to him, but he said he provided the boxes that the boys carried, so I didn't need the one my *bua* had given me. The boxes were twenty-litre cooking oil containers made of metal. He'd had a little door made in the top of each one. You could fit up to three hundred pieces into a box, but the little kids like me took only one hundred at a time. When one box was filled, the next boy in the line took it. So I needed to wait a while.

Then my turn came and the owner counted one hundred in front of me and gave me as many squares of newspaper. He showed me how to pick them up with the paper because customers don't like it if you touch them with your hand.

Then I followed the kid in front of me for a while, from a distance, to see what he did. As he was walking along the street, was shouting, "*Yeh ... kachori ... samosa ... garma garam!*" So I copied him. It was easier than I expected. In about three hours they were all sold, and I returned to the shop. I was planning to go home with my thirty rupees, but the owner asked if I wanted to sell one hundred more. By the afternoon I had earned sixty rupees. The owner said he trusted me now, so he also gave me back my deposit. He even gave me two free *samosas* to eat and a cup of *chai*. So I could give my grandmother back her money that same day, and I could give some money to my *bua*. Everybody was happy.

Within a couple of days I realised that by about 10 a.m. there were lots of boys out selling snacks on the streets. So I started going earlier than them in the morning. At 7:30, people were on their way to work, and who can resist a hot samosa for breakfast? Also, I started selling them in places that the other boys didn't go. They all stayed in the streets near to the shop, so there was lots of competition. But I would walk further. I'd sell them in video arcades, or near the big Sufi shrine where people were always coming and going.

It was really hard work. Sometimes I would work until late at night, but often I sold three or four hundred *kachoris* and *samosas* in a day. Then I could give lots of money to my *bua* and some to my sister. That was good, because when papa returned to Ajmer a couple of months later, he had saved absolutely nothing. He wanted me to stay in Ajmer permanently, but I said no. I told him the Pink City was my home.

I learned a lot in those weeks. I realised I didn't need a boss. I could work better as my own boss. And I learned that you needed to watch what everybody else was doing, and then do it better, or do something different so there was no competition.

◆ ◆ ◆

Winter was on the way, and the weddings were starting again. So at 7 in the evening, when the *chai* boss went home, I would eat quickly then go and do my second job, collecting things in the marriage gardens until 2 or 3 a.m. Then I could bring home food for the next day as well. I used to get about 4 hours of sleep at night, so I was always tired. But it was not every day. On the days that people were needed to work in the marriage gardens a *thekedar* – a contractor – used to organise it for them. He would travel around the city and find the right numbers of people that the different marriage gardens needed.

His name was Gopal, and I became quite friendly with him.

I knew that Gopal owned a couple of rickshaws. When it was off-season he sometimes pulled one himself, but he made plenty of money from organising workers for the marriage gardens so they were usually just locked.

I used to ask him over and over if he would let me rent one, sometimes as a joke, because I knew he would say no. He had all the usual reasons. You're too small. What if the police stop you?

Then one day, he just said, *"Theek hai."* I could hardly believe it. He had said okay, and he was serious. He handed me the keys and said, "You have to start somewhere. So start here."

I went to speak with the *chai* boss. Well, not immediately. It took me ages to build up the courage. I was really nervous because I was just a little kid and I knew he would be angry. He got angry about everything. I explained to him that we couldn't live on ten rupees a day and so I was going to leave and work for myself. I always spoke to him respectfully. And I needed to be careful because he knew Gopal, and he had a lot of influence. I was afraid he would tell Gopal to take back his rickshaw. Then I would have no job and no rickshaw. The *chai* boss was furious, and he shouted at me. He said if I was planning to leave I should have told him weeks ago so he could have found a replacement. Perhaps he was right. But I would have been more loyal to him if he had treated me well. He was so angry he told me I was fired, and I could leave right away. That suited me fine. I didn't want to stay a second longer than I had to. Later, when I thought about it, it seemed quite funny, or quite sad. I had quit, but he had wanted to make it look like he had fired me.

I'm not sure how old I was at the time. Ten ... eleven ... maybe twelve years of age. I had worked at the *chai* stall seven days a week, twelve-to-fourteen hours a day, for about three years. He had paid me as little as he could get away with, without us actually dying of starvation. It felt to me like papa's debts were well paid.

In a final attempt to be the tough boss, the *chai* boss sent somebody to tell us we were not allowed to sleep near to his *chai* stall any longer. But he didn't own the street, and he knew that all the rickshaw pullers were really on our side. He had turned people against him with his behaviour. So we ignored him. I'm sure that made him even more angry. Anyway, he wasn't in charge of our lives any longer and that felt good.

Now, when I tell you this, I sound very confident. But I wasn't at the time. I was really nervous and worried. All the time I was thinking, what will happen if I get no customers? What if I don't earn enough to even pay the rickshaw rent? Should I have just stayed at the *chai* stall? It would have been safer. At least we could eat *tari* and *chapattis* on 10 rupees a day. But I knew if it was going to work out, I needed to be confident and believe in myself. At least, I would have to pretend to be confident.

So each day I would cycle my rickshaw into the city. Some days I would get only one or two passengers, and they also used to pay very little money. I didn't know how to do it then. I used to tell the passengers, "I'm new here. I don't know how much to charge you to go to C-Scheme. You can pay me as you like." Sometimes they would give me almost nothing.

Before getting in, some would ask me over and over, "You do know how to drive it? You won't fall over or cause an accident?" I used to answer them with a lot of confidence. I'd say, "Nothing like that will happen. I'll drive, and I'll drop you at your destination. That's all. I've done this many times."

It got easier as I became more self-confident. Some days I would get two or three passengers. Then I could just about buy food and pay the rickshaw rent. But many times I didn't earn enough money for the daily rickshaw rent. So I used to tell Gopal, "I'll pay you double tomorrow or the day after." He understood that people were afraid because I was so small. He would say, "It's fine. When you have the money, you can pay me. There's no hurry."

Often I would go and sit near to the Jai club, waiting for a passenger, but not too close to the *chai* stall. A lot of people who came in the area knew me because I had worked there. So that helped. But still I needed to persuade them. They would say, "No, you're too young. You'll crash." When I'd taken them a couple of times they became convinced that I could cycle the rickshaw properly. Still, many times, on the way, they would be saying, "Drive carefully. There's no hurry. Drive over to the side of the road."

I used to drive slowly and near to the kerb so they wouldn't worry. Sometimes, if I was a bit desperate to get a passenger, I used say, "You can pay me half of the money you usually pay for the trip." Everybody knew approximately how much they would need to pay for a rickshaw. So if their fare home was usually 8 or 10 rupees, I would charge them 4 or 5. Sometimes the other rickshaw drivers would be angry with me for that. They would say, "Why do you make it so cheap? Next time they will expect that price from me too." But I used to say, "Passenger won't get into my rickshaw unless I'm cheaper than you. We need the money to eat." Some passengers would take pity on the little kid and pay me the full amount anyway when I got them safely to their destination.

Things started to get easier. Slowly I saved a little bit of money, and I started taking papa to see the *pahalwan* again. I used to take him three of four times a month, because I wanted him to start walking again. He hadn't walked for such a long time. He hadn't even tried. He just lay there in the street on that metal box.

For fifty rupees, the *pahalwan* would massage his legs and apply ointments. He said over and over that there was nothing wrong with papa's bones or muscles. Then slowly, slowly, I told papa, "If you can't walk, sit on my rickshaw and cycle for a short while. You need to get your jammed nerves opened. If you don't take exercise, you'll never be able to walk again."

At the start he used to have a lot of pain in his feet and he would say, "I can't do it. It's too difficult. My legs won't move."

But I used to push him. I'd tell him, "I know it hurts, but try. You've got to keep trying."

During that time I saved about three hundred rupees, and I told papa, "We have to go to Ajmer soon. It's been a very long time since we saw Raji." We hadn't seen her since before papa's accident. Maybe that helped a bit, because very slowly he started walking with the help of a stick.

During the daytime I was out looking for passengers. Before then I used to take him to the derelict house for his daily bathroom visit, but I told him, "When you need to go, you'll have to walk there on your own with your stick. I need to earn money for us." So he was forced to help himself.

Then one day I decided it was time to go to Ajmer. Obviously we both needed to take a shower and wash our clothes first. Then we took the 5 a.m. local train. The train was very cheap in those days. But by the time we had bought some presents to take and had given money to my *bua* and my sister, we were broke again, and so we returned to Jaipur by train without tickets.

In the train going home, we were sitting at the door near the toilet, so if the TTE came to check tickets, we could lock ourselves in the toilet. Doors are often left open on trains in India. It was a Sunday and a lots of young men were travelling home from somewhere after taking state exams to join the police force. The train was full, and so some of them were also sitting on the floor near the toilet. I had been listening to their conversations, comparing their answers to exam questions.

At about half way, the train stopped. It was hot and I was really thirsty, so I told papa, "I'm going to get out and drink some water here." He said, "No. Wait until we stop at a big station. This is a small one. The train won't stop here for long and there's already a queue for water."

I can be really stubborn sometimes, and so I insisted. I waited in line at the drinking fountain, and I wasn't really paying much attention to things. Besides being too stubborn, I know I also daydream too much. When my turn came to drink, I suddenly realised the train was already moving and my papa was hanging out of the door shouting for me to come. I started to run after it, but it was going too fast. I started shouting as well.

Then papa did something amazing. He threw his walking stick out of the train and he jumped out himself. He landed on his feet and he ran to me. The police cadets we had been sitting near to pulled the emergency chain and the train stopped up ahead. They all jumped out and made us get back in. Everybody was scolding me, saying things like, "Why did you get out? That was stupid!" And to my papa, "Are you mad, jumping out of a train? You could have fallen under it and been killed!" When we got in, they closed the train door to make sure we didn't do any other stupid things.

No harm was done, but from then on we were really afraid. The police cadets didn't realise we had no tickets. And we thought the TTE were sure to come and ask what the problem was and who had pulled the emergency chain. What would we say then? It was us who had made the train stop, and we didn't even have any tickets. Thankfully, they didn't come before we reached Jaipur. Perhaps because the train was so full.

But the thing is, at the time papa was still having difficulty walking with a stick. Then suddenly, when he needed to, he could jump out of a moving train.

When we arrived at Jaipur, since we had no money left, we had to walk from the train station. There was no choice. Papa had to walk with his stick back to our sleeping place. That was good, because it proved to him that when he needed to, he could walk all the way home as well as jump out of a train. From then on his health really started to improve.

◆ ◆ ◆

In those days, I never used to take passengers very far in my rickshaw. I'd only been a rickshaw puller for a few months and I didn't know the more distant parts of Jaipur. So if somebody wanted to go far I would refuse. It was a pity to turn customers away. Also I used to get very tired if I had two or three passengers together, so I couldn't go very far. I had grown a bit by then, so I could pedal the rickshaw properly if I stood on the pedals, but not if I sat on the seat. Then my legs were too short. So it took a lot of effort.

It was around then I discovered a new *dhaba*. It wasn't even a *dhaba*, there was no kitchen or seats. Everything was cooked over a fire on the footpath at the side of a road. You had to sit on the floor, or take the food with you. It was called Sethani ka Dhaba, and it was run only by ladies. They were always very friendly to me.

For three rupees I could buy a fantastic stuffed *paratha* with spicy vegetables. Even if you only bought a single *chapatti* for one rupee, they would give you vegetables with it for free. So even the poorest people could eat something good there. The *parathas* were big and thick. If I bought two of them, papa and I were already full.

They also made vegetable curry, and my favourite vegetable dish, *bhindi*, which is ladyfingers chopped and fried with chillies and peppers. The food that they cooked over a fire in the street was much better than the tourists ate at the fancy Indiana Restaurant for one hundred times more money. After so long eating *chapattis* and gravy, we were really happy to have good food again. If I had a few rupees to spare, I would also buy *beedis* for papa to smoke. But I would never, ever, buy alcohol for him.

Then in the evenings, the foreigners used to come to eat at the Indiana. Many would come by tuktuk and the drivers would wait outside to take them back to their hotels. I was familiar with the security guard, so I used to ask him, "Did any of the foreigners come here on foot? Can you let me know when they come back outside?" I used to park my rickshaw close to the gate. I had learned a few words of English by then, so when they came out I would say to them in English, "Please sit. I will take you."

I was still very young, and so they used to refuse. Maybe they were afraid to be driven by a child. Foreigners always think it's wrong for children to work. And they are correct. No children should have to work, and all children should go to school. But for some children it's not that simple. They work or they starve. Or they have to do much worse things than work to survive.

The older rickshaw drivers used to get annoyed with me. They would say, "What if you make the foreigners fall? If you have an accident, who will be responsible?" Or they would try, "Nobody is allowed to park their rickshaw right in front of the restaurant gate." But the security guard was my friend, and he decided what was allowed. So I used to ignore them. Then, a couple of times it happened. The older rickshaw pullers were not there, and I was lucky. The foreigners came out, and I said the English I had practiced, "Please sit. I will take you." And they said OK. But then I was stuck because I didn't know any more English. I used to ask the security guard to speak with them, or read the name of their hotel from a card. So he used to tell me, "This is the name of the hotel. The hotel is near this thing, or near that street. Ask somebody when you reach there." And he would tell the passenger it would be twenty or thirty rupees.

Sometimes I would get lost. I'd need to ask several people in the street how to find their hotel. When they realised I was lost, often the foreigners would get out and run away without paying. Some thought it was funny that I would need to keep stopping and asking. They were in no hurry, and so they enjoyed the trip. Others would give me my twenty or thirty rupees when I got lost and then stop a tuktuk to take them further. Most of them were nice. Sometimes they would give me a big tip for just a short journey. I always found it very interesting to pick up the foreigners, and I also used to think that I could learn something from them and earn more money at the same time.

When I used to take two or three foreigners at the same time, they would sit behind me and talk among themselves. So I used to keep my ears backwards while driving and I used to listen to them. I used to try to understand their words and I used to drive the rickshaw slowly. Sometimes I would catch one or two words. Then I'd repeat those words again and again in my head, and later I would ask to the security guard at the Indiana, "What does this mean?" He used to tell me, and I used to try to say those words correctly so I could use them next time I met foreigners.

Sometimes a foreigner would leave the restaurant and go on foot. They didn't want a taxi or tuktuk, they wanted to walk. Rich Indian people never walk anywhere unless it's very close, so that was always strange to me. But I also knew that foreigners always got lost in Jaipur. It's easy to get lost even when you live here. So I used to follow them, and after a kilometre or so, when they were tired or lost, I would say, "Please sit. I will take you."

Sometimes you don't need to understand a language to know what people are saying. They would be talking to each other. One would be saying, "Oh, that little boy has followed us for so long. Look at his clothes, he needs the money. Let's take his rickshaw." Another would be saying, "No. Look at him, he's just a child. He shouldn't be working." Often they didn't want to sit, but they would try to give money to me. They were always surprised when I refused it. I would be saying to them in Hindi, "I'm working. If you sit in my rickshaw, I'll take your money. Otherwise I don't want it. I'm not a beggar!"

◆ ◆ ◆

So, life started going better. We were still sleeping on the street, but I felt like I could take care of myself and also papa. I could pay the rickshaw rent, and earn fifty or sixty rupees a day, sometimes even more if I could get a foreign passenger from the Indiana. But I had underestimated how angry I had made mean old *Jallaad* the *chai* boss. Perhaps he hated to see me doing well.

Perhaps I annoyed him by picking up customers close to his *chai* stall, where his own rickshaw pullers were sitting around doing nothing. Whatever the reason, he now considered me to be his arch enemy. I could never understand why. He was a grown man, a rich man. And I was a street kid around his child's age, with nothing at all. I heard that he was always complaining to people about me. And he complained about my papa lying on the metal box in the street.

One day Gopal told me to park his rickshaw and give him the key. He said, "You'll need to rent a rickshaw from somebody else from now on. I can't let you use mine anymore." I was shocked. I told him, "I've driven your rickshaw for months now without any accidents or damage. I don't owe you any money. I pay you the rent on time. I also clean it daily. What's the problem?" He simply said, "I just can't let you use it anymore. That's all." I could see that he was ashamed of himself. He was a good person. He was the one who had given me a chance in the first place.

Nothing in that world stays secret for long. I heard that the *chai* boss had put pressure on him. I don't know exactly how. Maybe he knew the owners of the marriage gardens who employed Gopal as their *thekedar*. Whatever power he had over Gopal, he had made Gopal behave badly.

So I locked the rickshaw and handed him the key. But if the *chai* boss had expected me to crawl to him and beg for my old job back, he was mistaken. I would never give him that pleasure. The next day I was out collecting empty bottles again.

◆ ◆ ◆

During the previous months, I had got to know some people who owned rickshaws. I asked around, but none of them would agree to rent one to me. Then I started to ask for work at the rival *chai* stalls in the neighbourhood. One of them agreed to let me work there. He was called Kailash-ji. He said, "You can start tomorrow. But I won't pay you much at the start. And I won't let you serve my customers because you don't keep yourself clean. People expect the waiter to be neat and tidy, and you don't even take a shower." He would only let me collect and wash the glasses. I had no choice, so I agreed. He said he would pay me thirty rupees in the beginning, which at least was more than the mean old *Jallaad* used to pay me to do everything. So, at 7 a.m. the next day I was back to square one, washing *chai* glasses for twelve hours a day and collecting bottles at night.

Whenever I met somebody who owned a rickshaw, I used to say to them, "I'll pay you twenty-five or thirty a day instead of fifteen if you let me rent your rickshaw." But it was useless.

Again, there was no money to take papa to the *pahalwan*. And Kailash-ji was always on my back, saying things like, "You need to take a shower and change your clothes if you want to keep working for me." How could I afford to take a shower each day on a salary of thirty rupees?

When I had saved a bit of money, I went to a street market where they sold second-hand clothes and I bought a change of clothes so I could at least wash what I was wearing. That stopped my boss from complaining so much, but my employment at the new *chai* shop didn't last much longer.

Kailash-ji used to send me every hour to fetch milk from the dairy shop because he had no cooler. The shop was only fifty meters away. The milk guy was always making jokes when I was there, but that delayed me, and my boss would be annoyed if he ran out of milk and had to wait for me to return. So sometimes I had to tell the milk guy, "Please no jokes this time. I'm really in a hurry. I need you to give me the milk quickly so I can get back to work. My boss thinks I'm being lazy and wasting his time."

One day, not long after I had started, there were a lot of customers, and we were running out of milk, so Kailash-ji said, "Quickly go and fetch some milk." I ran to the dairy shop and asked for two litres of milk, and the milk guy started making jokes as usual. So I told him, "Please don't make any more jokes.

We have lots of customers waiting at the *chai* shop and I need the milk quickly."

I had probably hurt his feelings. His jokes were never funny and I had stopped pretending to laugh at them. Maybe he thought it would be funny to say, "I don't have any milk left. It's all sold." I knew it wasn't true, and I didn't think that was funny either. But what could I do? He refused to sell me any. That meant Kailash-ji had to go himself to fetch milk, and he returned with two litres. He said, "You told me he had no milk. Why?" I said, "The milk guy must have been joking or something. He told me it was finished." He said, "You're a liar," and he slapped me very hard across my face in front of all the customers. I didn't expect that from him. It made me cry, and I didn't want anybody to see that, so I ran down the road to get away from him.

It takes a brave man to hit a small child. But this is how children who work are often treated. It was normal. I knew that. I had seen many things and heard plenty of stories. I had had some bad bosses myself, but this was the first time my boss had ever hit me. And if somebody hits you once, they'll do it again. The mean old *Jallaad* probably would have hit me sometimes, but his legs had been chopped off by a train, so it wasn't easy for him to do.

Later, when I was feeling better, I walked back to the *chai* shop. Kailash-ji had calmed down by then, and when he saw me, he called me over. "Look, there were a lot of customers waiting," he said, "That's why I hit you. I was just angry, but it's over now. So get back to work."

Some people believe they have power over you. And they are always shocked when you show them that they don't. I had already learned that they only really have power over you if you give it to them. You can take that power away if you want to. It may go against you, but you can do it. So I said, "No. I'm finished here. I'll never work for you again." After all, I had quit one job recently. It was getting easier. But I stayed at a safe distance in case he tried to hit me again. He was so shocked that he didn't know what to say. And I walked away.

Along the road was another *chai* stall. I knew the owner, and I knew he had been looking for a boy to work there. I told him what had happened, and he immediately offered me a job working for him. There was a lot of rivalry between the *chai* stalls at that time. Perhaps it was good to take away your rival's workers. And everybody knew I was a hard worker. I told him I would work for him on the condition that I didn't ever have to fetch milk from the joker in the dairy shop. And he agreed to that.

The next day I also saw the milk seller in the street. It was a small neighbourhood, you bumped into everybody. He knew what had happened. He said, "He was just in a bad mood and he slapped you because there were customers waiting. I told him it was my silly joke. He needs help. He can't run the business on his own. Go back to work for him. Don't be childish." But like I've told you before, I can be very stubborn. And anyway, I was a child. I told him I would never go back to that *chai* shop, nor would I ever again come to his milk shop. Actually, in the end this wasn't true. He didn't apologise, but he was a good person, and I could tell he was really sorry for what he had caused with his joke. I forgave him, and he later became a good friend who helped me in a really important way. I'll tell you about that later.

So, I was back at the start yet again, working at yet another *chai* shop collecting glasses and washing them. The only problem was that this place stayed open until later. It closed at about 8:30. Work at the marriage gardens was still in full swing, but I finished too late to work there in the evenings. It was a pity, because there was a marriage garden called Mahaveer House less than half a kilometre away. When we were clearing up and washing things at the *chai* stall in the evening, I used to see the crowds of people walking down the street towards the entrance.

I noticed that whenever a marriage took place at Mahaveer House, a balloon seller used to come to sell coloured balloons and toys for the children in the street. He sold balloons for ten rupees each. I hadn't seen that at any of the other marriage gardens, and I thought maybe I could try it for myself. I had a bit of money saved, so after work, I bought a bag of balloons for forty rupees and found that there were forty balloons inside, so I could make up to nine rupees profit for every balloon I sold. Then, whenever there was a wedding, after work I used to inflate some balloons and sell them in the street when people were arriving. Sometimes I sold them for eight-fifty, sometimes for ten rupees. I only needed to sell four or five balloons to pay for our food from the Muslim *dhaba*.

◆ ◆ ◆

I've already told you about Pandit-ji, who worked at the Indiana Restaurant. He had brought food from the restaurant for papa and I when things were really bad for us. Well, when Pandit-ji heard I was working somewhere else, he started drinking *chai* where I worked instead of buying it from the mean old *Jallaad*. I use to speak with him often. If we were not busy, I used to sit with him for a while. He always had interesting things to tell me. My new boss was a nice man who was very quiet. I worked hard for him, and he never made any problems for me. But I didn't stay there for long.

One day I told Pandit-ji that the only way things could get better for papa and I would be if I could somehow rent another rickshaw. I didn't want to spend the rest of my life washing *chai* glasses and fetching bags of sugar, always fighting to earn just enough to eat, and sleeping in the street.

He knew a lot of people and he was respected because everybody knew he was educated and very intelligent. He had studied engineering at college and he could fix any broken machine. Pandit-ji told me he would ask around and see what he could do to help.

A few days later, he came to drink *chai*, and told me he had arranged for me to rent another rickshaw. The owner wasn't happy renting it to such young kid, but Pandit-ji had told him that he trusted me so much, if anything happened to the rickshaw, he would be responsible for it himself.

◆ ◆ ◆

Our fortune had changed once again with the help of Pandit-ji. I could save a little money, and I started taking papa back to the *pahalwan*. I decided I had to always drive very carefully so there were never any problems.

It was still difficult for me because I was small for my age, so I never took passengers very far. With time and treatment, papa's health was improving. I used to make him exercise by cycling an empty rickshaw for thirty minutes or an hour every day. Occasionally he even started taking a passenger, but he was still very weak, so I would sit on the back so I could get out and push if we came to a hill. The more papa moved, the better his legs got. I could see him improving every day.

Then we started to work in shifts. Papa pulled the rickshaw during the day, and after we had eaten in the evening, I would work until midnight. As my English improved, I found it easier to get foreign passengers from the Indiana. But there was no point in me sitting doing nothing all day. I asked around and found somebody who would rent me another rickshaw for papa. With two rickshaws, we could both earn money during the daytime, and it seemed like our problems were finally solved.

Papa had not drunk much alcohol for a very long time. That was because I controlled the money. Sometimes some of the rickshaw pullers would feel sorry for him lying on that box in the street, and they would bring him a small bottle of wine. But I would never buy liquor for him. I had known many addicts by then. It doesn't matter if it's *doda* or heroin or alcohol that they use. They may stop for a time, but they usually start again. You can never really trust them when they need drugs.

Papa was away from me most of the day with his own

rickshaw, and he now controlled his own money, so his old habits quickly came back. Soon, whatever he earned he would spend on liquor. It was even easier for him now I was working. He didn't need to worry about me anymore. Sometimes we would eat together, but often he would buy booze and food for himself, and he would eat and get drunk somewhere away from me, where he didn't have to listen to my complaints. I used to earn less than him because I was young, and passengers were still reluctant to sit in my rickshaw. I would earn maybe fifty to eighty rupees a day. I used to say to him, "Please don't do this again. You need to save some money. We have to think about Raji. She lives in your sister's house and we should pay her expenses. And we need to save because she is getting to marriageable age now." In India, the family of the bride always have to pay for the wedding.

He used to say. "Yes, yes, okay." But his habits only got worse, and he started to drink away everything he earned as soon as he earned it.

◆ ◆ ◆

Again, it had been a long time since we had been to Ajmer to visit Raji. After I had worked all day, I would sit outside the Indiana Restaurant hoping to get a foreign passenger in the evening, so I could save the extra money for us to visit.

Then one day a foreigner came out of the Indiana. He told me he didn't want a rickshaw and he started walking. I followed him. My English was getting better, so I said to him, "I will drop you. Where do you want to go?" He continued to refuse, but he stayed friendly and smiled at me.

Eventually, I thought he was lost, but he wasn't. He was looking for a shop. Then he called me over and said, "I want to buy some alcohol for a *Holi* party. Do you know anywhere nearby I can get it?" I took him to one of those expensive fancy wine shops where the tourists go. He bought some bottles of wine and beer. Then he gave me his hotel card and asked, "Do you know where this is?" I couldn't read the card, but still I told him, "Yes okay, I know." I was lucky. I started cycling in the direction he had been walking and he knew the way. He said, "Yes, I came from this way. Go straight." He was talking a lot in English that I couldn't understand, but showing me with hand gestures to go left or right.

It was just 2 days before *Holi*. In India that's a big festival, like Christmas. The shops all close. People have parties with their friends and family, and they throw coloured powder over each other. I was thinking how nice it would be to visit Raji for the festival. But it was impossible with papa drinking away every rupee he earned.

Then we were at the hotel. It had been easy. I told the man he owed me thirty rupees and he handed me a five-hundred rupee note. That was a problem. I said, "Sorry, I have no change." Sometimes foreigners would try to pay for a twenty rupee ride with a one-hundred rupee note. And they would think I was trying to cheat them when I said I had no change. They'd think, 'It's just a hundred rupees. That's only a euro! Everybody can change that.' They didn't understand. Sometimes I had no money at all. Most days I didn't earn one hundred rupees in total.

But this man didn't get angry. He smiled and said, "It's OK. Keep the change. Happy *Holi!*" Then he walked into his hotel with his bags full of bottles.

I don't think I had ever held a five hundred rupee note before. I'd certainly never owned one. It was a crisp, clean, new one. Right out of an ATM. It was beautiful. Now you may think, 'That's only six or seven dollars.' But I jumped for joy because of what it would allow us to do.

I went straight back to tell papa that we could go and visit Raji at *Holi*. So we went to Ajmer for the weekend. We could take sweets as presents, give some money to my *bua*, and buy tickets for the train as well. I felt like I was rich.

Chapter 5: The day I nearly died in the holy lake

While we were in Ajmer during *Holi*, my *bua* mentioned marriage again. She had mentioned it to me many times before. She said, "Raji is getting to the age now when she'll need to get married. Your father doesn't care about this, but you're her brother. You have a duty to save money to pay for it." This was correct, and I started to worry about it. What would happen if there was no money available when the time came for Raji to get married? I knew I needed to start saving for her wedding.

I mentioned to you that my friend, the security guard at the Indiana Restaurant, used to act as a bank for lots of the street people. Each day I started to deposit whatever money was left over with him. Usually just ten or twenty rupees, but sometimes even fifty or more if I'd had a good day. Then, when I had about one thousand rupees saved, every one or two months, I used to go alone to Ajmer to meet my sister, and I would give the money to my *bua* to keep safe for Raji's wedding. I didn't tell my papa about this, and he didn't notice that I was gone.

Having a bank account with the security guard was good. He was a trustworthy person. If I had a bad day, I knew I always had some money saved to pay my rickshaw rent and buy food.

I also became more confident. Instead of waiting for a passenger, I started roaming up and down the M.I. Road. Did I tell you why it's called the M.I. Road? It's really called the Mirza Ismail Road, but nobody likes saying that, so everybody says M.I. Road. Anyway, there were always lots of foreign tourists there who were usually on foot. There were also expensive restaurants, and the only bar in the city centre that wasn't part of a hotel. Often I would wait outside a restaurant or the Bouncer

Bar until after midnight hoping to pick up a tourist. Of course, there was a lot of competition. If a foreigner handed me a hotel card I would have to ask somebody to read it to me. So there was a delay. Then the tuktuk drivers who were also waiting there would tell the tourist in English, "Look at him, he's just a little kid. He's had many accidents with that rickshaw. If you want to be safe in the traffic, then you'd better come with me instead. Otherwise you might get killed by a car." I used to lose many customers that way.

So I found a way around that. I would ask the tourist to sit, and then drive away from the restaurant. When I saw a well-dressed, educated-looking Indian person, I would stop and say in Hindi, "Excuse me sir, can you help this foreign visitor please? Can you read this card and tell me where this person wants to go?" And they would usually say something like, "Oh yes, they want to go to the Sheraton."

Although I couldn't read – even in Hindi – I knew that I needed to learn to speak better English. That would be a key to my future. Most of the rickshaw pullers could speak no English at all. And most couldn't read or write at all in Hindi. I needed an advantage.

Pulling that rickshaw, I invented lots of tricks. Sometimes I would get a couple of really heavy foreigners who were difficult to pull. You can usually tell if somebody is going to be fun or not. If it was a fun person, I would joke with them and say, "Phew! It's very difficult. You try?" Often they would say yes. Then I would steer and let them pedal. Or some would even make me sit in the seat and they would drive. Of course they always wanted a photograph to show people back home. When they understood how hard it was to pull a rickshaw they often gave me a big tip, even if they had done all the work.

Then one day I was listening to a tuktuk driver speaking to some foreigners. They gave him a hotel card and said, "We want to go here." The driver couldn't read English, so he handed the card back to them and said, very clearly, "Can you read this to me please?" That was it! That was the question I needed. I practised it over and over in my head. And it worked. The next time a tourist handed me a card, I said, "Can you read this to me please?" And they said, "Sure. It says hotel Arya Niwas." By then I knew the names and locations of most of the hotels in Jaipur, so it became easy.

There were other tricks. I noticed that tourists would choose a rickshaw that was nicely decorated, because they wanted a photograph of themselves sitting in it. So I decorated my rickshaw, and I would tell them, "I can take photograph if you want." They would often give me a tip for doing that. All the spare money got saved for my sister's wedding.

◆ ◆ ◆

In Ajmer, my *bua* started looking for a match for my sister. When I used to go every one or two months with money, I would hear about it. My *bua* used to say, "It won't take long before we've found a boy to marry your sister. We'll get her married any time now. As soon as a good match is found." Most marriages in Rajasthan are still arranged by parents. They choose who their son or daughter marries.

Since all of my spare money went toward the marriage, I still wore my torn old clothes. My *bua* didn't like this. She used to say, "At least when you come for the wedding be sure to wear some new clothes." So I'd tell her, "Yes, I'll get some good clothes when I'm back in Jaipur."

It really didn't take long. One day my *bua* found a boy to marry Raji. He was a good match, she said, and she arranged for them to get married without even telling papa or me. When I visited to give money, she showed me his photo, and she said, "We'll decide on the date of the wedding soon. It'll be in about three or four months." It was to be a communal wedding at the *sammelan*. This is when a lot of people get married at the same time. Rich people contribute the costs so that poor people can get married. This was much less expensive than having a private wedding. Only clothes and some silver jewellery for the bride would need to be bought. And a small celebration party would have to be paid for afterwards.

When I was back in Jaipur, I told my papa about it. I hoped it would make him take things seriously and start to save, but it didn't. Whatever money he earned, he used to spend on liquor. And he was back to his other old habit. At night, when he would drink too much, he wouldn't sleep. He used to shout all night, and pick fights with people for no reason. I was really fed up with all these things, and I started sleeping a bit away from him in my rickshaw, further down the street.

Then, suddenly, the day of the wedding was approaching fast. I wanted to go to Ajmer a few days before the wedding. So I kept telling papa, "Your daughter's getting married. We need to go to Ajmer." And he'd say, "Yes, yes, we'll go." But he didn't seem interested at all, and he would drink, and drink.

Then it was the day before the wedding. My father had saved nothing at all. So I took all my savings from the security guard at the Indiana. I had about 700 rupees in total. I planned to buy some second-hand clothes when I arrived in Ajmer because I was still wearing my old worn-out ones.

By then I'd had enough of it, so I told my papa, "I am going to Ajmer today. If you want to come with me, get ready. Otherwise stay here." Finally, he agreed. When we arrived at the station in Jaipur, he said, "First give me the rest of the money you've saved. I need a drink." I'd already given him half of my savings to buy the tickets and some clothes for himself.

That was the first time that I really had a fight with my papa. I knew if he had all the money he'd get drunk and we would miss the wedding completely. So we shouted at one another.

I was so angry, I left him outside the station. I went and bought a ticket to Ajmer for myself and I sat in the train. After a few minutes, the TTE came along. I had travelled so many times with papa without a ticket. This time, at least, I had one. But when you're angry and upset, you make stupid mistakes. And as I told you before, I daydream too much. Sometimes I'm so busy with what's happening inside my head I don't see what's happening around me. The TTE inspector said, "This is a ticket for the local train. You're in the high-speed express train. You'll need to pay a fine."

I told him I had only 250 rupees, and I needed that because I was on the way to my sister's wedding. He said, "You either pay the fine, or I fetch the police and then you'll spend three months in jail. It's up to you."

I told him that it wasn't deliberate. I had only made a mistake. And I pleaded with him. I said, "It's my sister's wedding today. Please just let me go. Otherwise I'll miss it." He took me to an office in Ajmer station, and I had to give him all the money I had in my pockets to be allowed to leave. It wasn't an official fine, that was clear. There was no paperwork or forms. He kept the money for himself. But, at least, I wouldn't miss the wedding. Then I had to walk all the way to my *bua*'s house, and so I arrived for the wedding with no money and wearing my usual dirty, worn-out clothes. When I explained what had happened, my *bua* became angry. She said, "Well, it's your own fault for being so stupid."

She had two sons, one younger and one older than me. I asked if I could borrow some of their clothes to wear, because I couldn't go to the wedding looking like I did. But she only scolded me again. She said, "Where do you think we'll get clothes from for you? We've been looking after your sister for many years. And now you want us to give clothes to you. Well, we haven't got any clothes for you. So you'll have to go looking like that." It was really unfair. The reason my clothes were old was because I had worked and saved for the last year to pay for Raji's wedding. My money had probably even paid for the new clothes my *bua* was wearing for the wedding.

So I went to the wedding in the evening wearing my normal clothes. My jeans were dirty and there was a hole near to the zip at the front, and I had a pair of worn-out old flip-flops on my feet. The best I could do was to clean my shirt during the afternoon and wash my hair. I tried to look happy for Raji. It was her wedding day. But all the time I was crying inside.

When the ceremony was over, I was talking to Raji, and her new husband's parents came over and asked, "Who is he?"

Raji said, "This is Naresh. He's my brother." Then, while we were talking, like a scene from a Bollywood comedy film, my papa arrived. He was furious and drunk. He told Raji he had missed her wedding because I had left him at the station in Jaipur. That wasn't true. I'd given him half of my money. He could easily have bought a train ticket himself. There were many trains to Ajmer he could have got.

Then Raji's new father-in-law asked, "And who is he?"

"He's my father," Raji said.

Her parents-in-law both looked shocked. It was not only because of our appearance. As you can imagine, we didn't make a good impression. But we found out later that during the wedding negotiations, my *bua* had told them that she and her husband were Raji's parents. It would have made Raji seem more attractive as a bride to have respectable parents.

I felt completely humiliated. I could tell they were looking at me, dressed in my dirty worn-out clothes, and looking at papa, who was drunk and angry, and was also wearing the stinking, filthy old clothes that he slept in. I could see them thinking, 'Why would they come to the wedding dressed like that? What kind of family is this?'

But still, they said, "On the day of the wedding, according to our customs, we also take the younger brother of the bride along with us to stay overnight. So Naresh should come with us to our house."

After the short celebration, they took me along with my

sister to their home. They gave me food and a place to sleep. The next day they bought some new clothes for me, one day too late.

All the time I was trying to look happy for Raji's sake. But still, inside, I was crying. I felt ashamed. After all my work, after all the money I had saved to pay for the wedding, I had arrived with no wedding present for my sister, and I had embarrassed her in front of her new family. But I told myself, the most important thing was that my sister had got married after all. She was no longer dependent on my *bua*, and she didn't need to worry any more about papa not sending money for her expenses.

After taking a shower, I put on the new clothes, and went to my *bua*'s house to say goodbye. I sat there for a while feeling uncomfortable. Then I came back to Jaipur without my papa. We were not speaking to one another. It was first time that had ever happened. And I thought he could make his own way back to Jaipur when he was ready. After all, he was the adult, and I was the child.

According to another Hindu tradition, as the younger brother of the bride, I had been given some money by my new brother-in-law. So I could buy a train ticket. And I made sure I was on the local train this time. It's really difficult to find the right train when you can't read.

Sitting in the train back to Jaipur, I thought a lot. Now Raji's future was safe. She had a husband to look after her. I had looked after my papa for so many years and nursed him all the time he was sick. My family had always been very important to me. And I knew they always would be. But I decided that now I had to try to do something for myself, for my own future.

◆ ◆ ◆

For days after I got back to Jaipur, whenever I thought about the wedding, and nobody could see me, tears came to my eyes. And for the first time in my life, I was extremely angry with papa. And I stayed angry for a long time. He came back to Jaipur a couple of days after me.

At night, I started sleeping somewhere away from him, but it was difficult to sleep because it was new place for me, and I was scared to sleep alone in the street. I was still just a young kid and I had heard so many stories of really bad things happening to kids.

So a few days later, I went back to sleeping at our old place in front of the Indiana Restaurant. But papa's drinking was worse than ever. It was out of control, and that changed him. Whenever he had money to drink at night, he wouldn't sleep, but he would yell all night long. So I also couldn't sleep. Sometimes, if there was nobody to fight with, he would aim his anger at me, and hit me for no reason. Again I started to sleep a couple of streets away in my rickshaw, but late at night when it was quiet, I could still hear him shouting. Then he would come looking for me, and when he found me he would get angry and start hitting me. A couple of times I had to leave my rickshaw behind and run to get away from him.

He would just shout all night without any reason, waving a fist as if he was angry at the stars. I did my best to silence him, but it was as if he didn't understand me, like the drink made him a different person. I was also scared that the police might come and take papa away if somebody complained about him. Then, in the morning, I used to sleep for a few hours under tree somewhere far away where he wouldn't find me.

I started staying away from the Indiana Restaurant during the daytime while I was looking for customers. Then I would check that papa had food in the evening, and I'd sleep a couple of kilometres away, near to other people if possible.

I started to wonder if I should leave Jaipur. Leave everything and everybody behind, and start again somewhere new. But I was still a child, with nobody – except papa – to support me. Where could I go? I didn't know anybody. My mother's parents had been quite wealthy, or so I had heard. They used to live in Gujarat. I didn't even know if they were still alive. When my mother passed away, my papa didn't tell them. He said he had had no way to contact them. They found out later that their daughter was dead from somebody else. So they didn't go to her funeral. They never forgave papa for that, and so I didn't think they would make me very welcome.

My biggest problem was that I had no documents. I had no ID card. There was not a single paper to even prove that my name was Naresh. So how could I go somewhere and start again? Without an ID, I could do nothing. I couldn't have a normal job with a contract, or rent a room. I couldn't have a bank account. I couldn't get a driving license or a passport. Because, according to the government, I didn't even exist, and you needed an ID for all of those things.

◆ ◆ ◆

I still used to keep a lookout for foreigners. I was always interested in foreigners, and my English was improving by the day. The more I listened to people speaking English, the more it started to make sense to me.

One night outside Niro's Restaurant on the M.I. Road I met two Japanese boys. They were both around twenty years old. As usually happened, they gave me their hotel card and I asked them to read it to me. They were funny, and very friendly, but very different from each other. Miki had short hair and wore neat clothes. He looked like a film actor and he had an important job in Japan. He seemed to have a lot of money and he was always paying far much too much for things. Yoske was a student. He looked pretty ordinary. He was thin and had very long black hair. He wore simple cotton clothes that always looked a bit too big for him. From the back you could easily have mistaken him for a girl. They both had big touch-screen mobile phones that could take photographs. At the time such phones were very unusual in India. They also had expensive-looking cameras with them.

They told me that rickshaws had been invented in Japan and that the Hindi name *riksha* was actually a Japanese word. But they didn't have rickshaws in Japan any longer.

When I dropped them at their hotel, I asked if they would like me to take them on a tour of the Pink City the next day. Tourists always used to say no when I asked this, but they said, "Yes, OK."

The next morning I picked them up outside their hotel. They came out of the hotel exactly at the time we agreed. And I showed them around the Pink City. They were really nice, and they asked if they could book me for the next few days. This was great for me. I had never had a customer for more than a single day before. So I took them all around Jaipur. I showed them everywhere in the Pink City and also around modern Jaipur. They were interested in everything, from the palaces and temples to the *dosa* sellers and *lassi* stalls. They drank a lot of *chai*. They also smoked a lot of drugs, which they had bought in Delhi and brought with them to Jaipur. We became friends. Most tourists were much older than me, but they were quite young, and that made a difference.

They always asked me to eat with them at lunch time and in the evening. I always made an excuse because I was too shy to go into the kind of fancy restaurants that they liked. But sometimes they bought street food and we ate together outside in my rickshaw.

Because I couldn't go very far with my rickshaw, they went by tuktuk one day to visit the fort at Amber. When they came back, they told me that they had talked about their plans. Miki needed to go back to Delhi. He had to return to work and his flight to Japan was in a couple of days. But Yoske wanted to stay in Jaipur for another week because he liked it so much. His flight back to Japan was later.

So I roamed around Jaipur with Yoske for another couple of days. He didn't really do anything, he just hung around, watched people and looked at things. He never drank alcohol, but he used a lot of drugs. He had a shiny brown ball of something in a small plastic bag, and he used to break bits off it and put them into the cigarettes that he rolled. He would smoke them in the back of my rickshaw while we were roaming around the city. It smelled a bit like *ghanja*, but it wasn't. Lots of street people smoked *ghanja*. That was plant leaves that people smoked in a *chillum* pipe. I also knew what *hashish* was. I had seen plenty of people using that too. But this was something different.

When I asked him what it was, he said, "It's called *charas*." I had never heard of *charas* before. He told me it had been made in India for thousands of years by a very old process. He said it was much better than *ghanja* or *hashish*. But it was also much more expensive.

Then one day he told me he had a plan to go to Ajmer and Pushkar. He knew I had been born in Ajmer, and he asked, "Can you come with me?" I told him I didn't know Ajmer as well as I knew Jaipur, but I could show him around the main tourist sites. And I thought, why not, it might be fun.

So the next day we took the bus to Ajmer. Just a local bus, not the kind of A.C. bus that tourists usually take. He had booked a room in a simple guesthouse in Ajmer on a very busy street near to the Sufi *Dargah*, and he wanted me to stay there with him. I had told him very clearly that I didn't have an ID card. In India, according to the law, you are not allowed to stay at a hotel if you have no ID.

When we arrived, the guesthouse owner explained this again to him. But Yoske said he would pay extra for me to stay. The guesthouse owner said, "And what will happen if there is a problem with the police?" Yoske said, "There will be no problems. It will be my responsibility if anything happens."

So we checked in. I had never stayed at a guesthouse before. At the time I thought it was very luxurious, because entire families lived in smaller rooms than that one, and it even had a private bathroom. But now I know it wasn't really fancy. It was a simple, dark room without A.C. It just had an electric *punkah* fan.

Yoske needed to be careful with money.

I showed Yoske around Ajmer for a couple of days. Then he wanted to go to Pushkar. That's a small town close to Ajmer. You can visit it easily from Ajmer in a single day. It's known as a holy town. In India there are three main gods: Shiva, Vishnu, and Brahma. Hindus worship Shiva and Vishnu at thousands of temples all over the country. But they say there is only one real Brahma temple in the whole world, and that's at Pushkar. There is also a holy lake, which was created by Brahma, and has been there for thousands of years.

So we took the bus to Pushkar. We walked around the town and visited the temples and markets. He really wanted to see the famous Brahma temple. Then I took him near to the holy lake. There are *ghats* at the edge of the lake where people bathe or wash their hands and face. Yoske asked why they were doing that, and I told him that washing in the holy lake at Pushkar washed away all your sins, just like bathing in the Ganges at Varanasi did. It also made you feel good. It was like having a *dharshan*, which is when you see God in something.

He had his big, expensive camera with him. He was always taking photos and he wanted to photograph the lake. But I explained to him that it was forbidden to take photographs of the holy lake. If he was seen doing that, he would get into a lot of trouble. Also, when you approached the lake, you had to take off your shoes. There was an announcement through loudspeakers telling you about the rules every few minutes.

It was almost time for us to go back to Ajmer. I told Yoske that I'd like to wash my hands and face in the lake to get rid of my sins, and asked if he also wanted to. He said, "No, no, I don't want to do that. I haven't committed any sins yet that are bad enough to wash away." But really, I think he was scared because the water looked green and dirty. He was always washing his hands and rubbing gel into them.

So I made him sit far away, where he could still wear his shoes and wouldn't get into any trouble, and went to wash my hands and face in the holy water. I took off my flip flops as I approached the lake. It felt really slimy as I went down the steps of the *ghat* towards the water. Because it was early evening, there was nobody around.

About four or five steps from the water's edge, my foot slipped on some mud. I slid down the other steps and fell into the lake. Even near to the edge, it was too deep for me to stand up, and I didn't know how to swim at the time. I sank and came to the surface for air coughing and splashing. I swallowed lots of the green holy water. Then I sank again.

It was strange, because although I was in a panic, my mind was quite clear. I was thinking that maybe today would be the last day of my life. Perhaps it would all end here. And I wondered, if I died here, who would tell my father and my sister? They didn't know I was in Pushkar. And I thought, I have no ID. According to the government, I don't even exist. Nobody knows who I am. Maybe Yoske wouldn't even realise what had happened. He would think I had left without him, and he would go back to his guesthouse alone. Then he'd go back to Japan and forget about me. Later the police would find my body in the lake, but they wouldn't know who I was or where I was from. To them, I would be another dead street kid. My body would be thrown on a funeral pyre, along with all the other nameless dead people who were found in the streets.

So many thoughts were running through my mind in slow motion. I thought of my life so far. And I thought: was that it? Those thirteen years, always fighting to survive, was that my life? I hadn't even had a chance to do anything interesting yet. I had just barely managed to exist. I had been a slave for most of the time, wasting my time working for free so other people could make money.

Then I thought I should try to swim like they do in the movies. With my mouth closed, I moved my hands and feet like I had seen in many films at the cinema, but it didn't work.

Even more than drowning, I was afraid because I knew the

lake was full of snakes. I thought I might get bitten by a water snake. They are very dangerous and poisonous, and I'm terrified of all snakes. Were there even any crocodiles? I wasn't sure.

It all seemed to take a long time, drowning in the holy water of the lake at Pushkar. Then my lungs were full of water, and I became very calm as I felt my death approaching. Actually, I felt quite happy that it was the end. All the problems and struggles would soon be over. It felt good. So I stopped fighting, and I decided to let death take me away.

Then something grabbed my foot. A snake! A water snake! Suddenly I had energy again. I panicked and I kicked it away. Then something grabbed my hand. But it wasn't a snake, it was a person.

What I didn't know was that a man who was selling marigold flowers at a stall had noticed me splashing about. He had jumped into the lake after me. He pulled me to the side and out of the water. I couldn't breathe because so much water had got into my lungs. The man lay me on the floor and climbed on my back to push the water out of my lungs. I was coughing and choking. Somebody fetched me a towel. By then a crowd was gathering around. Everybody was asking, "What happened little boy? Where are your parents?"

Yoske hadn't seen any of this. He had been sitting playing with his camera the whole time. Somebody went and told him, "The guide who came with you slipped in the water and nearly drowned." Then he came running. My clothes were soaked. Somebody said, "Take off your clothes and put this towel around you until they are dry."

An old lady who had been watching said, "You very nearly died. From now on, you have a new life. You should thank the flower seller for giving it to you." When I was feeling a little better, I touched the feet of the flower seller, and I thanked him for giving my life back to me. He just said, "It's no problem. It's not the first time I've done this. A lot of people fall into the lake. If I see them in the water, I try to save them. I'm a good swimmer.

But many people have drowned here in Pushkar."

I put my damp clothes on and we took the bus back to Ajmer. Sitting in the bus, Yoske kept asking me, "Are you OK? Are you OK?" He was worried about me. He also knew that he could have got into trouble for letting me stay in his room if I had died and the police had got involved. And he knew that ball of *charas* in his pocket was against the law. He must have realised he didn't want to have any problems with the police.

I told him that when we got back to the guest house, he mustn't tell the guest house owner what had happened, because they would kick me out. And Yoske would probably be kicked out as well. He said he understood. But I guess he was afraid. When I went to the room to change my clothes, he told the owner what had happened.

As I expected, I was asked to leave. The guest house owner said, "I'm sorry, I can't let you stay here anymore, because you don't have an ID card. If an accident happens, then my guest house will be closed down by the police, and this poor Japanese boy will also be in trouble."

So I said, "Okay, no problem. If you feel like that then I'll go." Joske said he would stay a couple more days in Ajmer, and he would meet me when he returned to Jaipur. But he never did.

◆ ◆ ◆

Back in Jaipur, I asked my papa about my birth certificate. If I had my birth certificate, I could get an ID card. He told me, once again, that it was somewhere at my *bua*'s house in Ajmer. That's where I had been born.

I knew that getting an ID card would be necessary if I was ever going to escape from living on the street, so one day I went back to Ajmer to ask my *bua* to search her house again. She told me she had looked many times, but she had never found it. Probably, when I was born in Ajmer, my papa didn't register my birth at all. He wasn't good at arranging things. So there never was a birth certificate. My sister Raji also had no birth certificate.

So I walked to the law court in Ajmer. I had been told there was a free lawyer who gave advice to poor people. At least the first advice was free. If you needed him to do anything for you, he charged a lot of money. The lawyer told me it was possible to get a simple ID card without a birth certificate, but I would need an electricity bill or water bill from the address where I lived, plus a copy of the IDs of the other people who lived there. But my *bua* refused to help me with this. She said, "We have no idea what you do or where you live. You can't give the address of our house as your address. What if you get into trouble with the police? Then they'll come knocking on my door." I asked my bua's husband, but he also refused. And my cousin, my *bua*'s eldest son, refused to help as well.

Finally I went back to Jaipur feeling really disappointed. I couldn't understand why they would refuse to help me. It seemed like a small thing to do to make such a big difference in my life.

◆ ◆ ◆

For a time, I started doing catering work full-time at a wedding garden. I would start at 8 or 9 a.m., and I would usually get free at 2 or 3 a.m. the next day, sometimes even 4 or 5 a.m. But it wasn't every day, so when I had no work the next day, I would sleep somewhere under a tree for most of the day. But I kept my rickshaw as well, and paid the daily rent. They had difficulty to get enough people to work during the daytime before the weddings started, so the pay was much better than working only at night.

Most of my friends at that time were rickshaw pullers. I hadn't had any friends of my own age for a long time. My friends were all more than twenty years older than me, and most of them were drunks or drug addicts, or both. Addicts are always happier when everybody around them is an addict too, so many times they used to push me to try drugs, even though I was still just a child. But I knew that if I started, in twenty years' time, I would be one of them. I'd be another addict, working to buy drugs before food. Then I would sleep in the street for the rest of my life. And one night, I would die alone in the street, like all the addicts do in the end.

Working at the marriage garden, I started to make some friends who were closer to my own age. One was called Ajay. He was about 20 years old. He was a high-caste Rajput, and from his appearance he once used to belong to a good family. But he had no family at all now, or so he said. His father had drunk himself to death. That was about all he would ever tell me about his background. I knew he was married to a girl who was a balloon seller. But it wasn't an arranged marriage like my sister Raji's had been, it was what we call a 'love marriage' in India. Perhaps that was why a high-caste boy had ended up living on the streets. Who knows.

From what he told me, the love hadn't lasted very long. He used to say, "My wife beats me and humiliates me in front of people." At one point Ajay rented a room, but his wife had always lived on the street, and she didn't like sleeping indoors, so she made him move back to their spot in the street. He told me his wife was always pressurizing him to earn more and more money. Sometimes he pulled a rickshaw, and sometimes he did catering work together with his wife's brothers. When they worked at the marriage garden, they used to steal lots of food and drink. He said it was because there wasn't work every day, so they needed to take enough food for several days.

When I was a little kid, I also used to steal plates of food from a marriage garden, but what Ajay and his wife's brothers did was different. They used to take big cans of cooking oil, bags of sugar, and sacks of flour. They would hide them early morning when they arrived at work, and would sneak them out in a rickshaw late at night. It was enough food to cook for weeks. And they used to sell the oil and flour to people to earn more cash. He was always telling me, "You should take things as well. They don't even notice it." But I was afraid, so I never took more than we were allowed to take home. Just food that was left over at the end of the night. Maybe sometimes I took too much *gulab jamun*. I really couldn't resist those sweet, sticky balls. But that was all.

Ajay was not the most honest friend. But it was good to know somebody who was not an old drunk or a drug addict. And I knew that if I had a problem, Ajay would always help me out.

◆ ◆ ◆

While I was working at the marriage garden I also got to know Aazad. He was a Muslim and a few years older than me. Aazad used to do the same work as me, which was picking up plates, washing things, collecting glasses, and generally clearing garbage from the garden to prepare for the marriage party in the evening. There was always a lot to do. Even a normal wedding has about two-thousand guests. Some have four or five thousand. Some people invite their entire village.

Aazad also pulled a rickshaw, and we used to meet on the M.I. road sometimes when there was no work at the garden. He used to sleep in his rickshaw near to McDonald's at *Panch Batti*, just around the corner from the Raj Mandir cinema. If I saw him there at night, I used to stop to talk to him. Often I would sleep in my rickshaw next to his. I still didn't want to sleep near to papa, and it was always safer to sleep near to somebody who I knew.

One evening, we were both lying in our rickshaws talking before going to sleep. A big foreign car – a BMW or an Audi – pulled up next to us. The driver sat there for a while looking at us through the window and then got out. It was a lady. She was about forty or fifty and she looked very rich. It was really unusual to see a rich lady driving her own car, especially in Jaipur. They always had a driver to do that for them.

She said, "There is some work to be done at my house and

I'm looking for a strong boy to take care of it for me." It was late and we were both tired after working all day, so neither of us was interested in going to carry heavy boxes or something. Then she said, "I'll pay you three hundred rupees for just a small job." Of course we both became interested at that point. But she didn't want us both to come. She pointed at Aazad and said, "No. I just want the bigger one."

She told Aazad he should lock his rickshaw and get into her car. She said she would drop him back here when the work was finished. It seemed very strange to me at the time, because rich ladies don't ever invite street boys into their expensive cars. And certainly not at night. I had never sat in any kind of car up to then. If it had been a man, I'm sure Aazad would not have gone. But a rich middle-aged lady surely couldn't be dangerous.

It was about 5 a.m. when Aazad returned. He woke me up and he was quite upset. He said, "She took me to a big house. We had to drive through a gate to get to it. It seemed empty. She took me into the kitchen and gave me a glass of orange juice. I told her I didn't want any, but she ordered me to. She said, 'drink it!' Then she sat next to me and started touching me. I started feeling very strange. I stood up and told her I wanted to go back to my rickshaw, but she told me to sit down. She said, 'If you don't do what I say, I'll tell the police you broke in and tried to rape me. And who do you think they will believe, me or a street boy?' Then she made me take off all my clothes and follow her into a bedroom. I was frightened because there was a wall around the house. It would be difficult to escape, and if the police came they might put me in jail for life. First she touched me a lot and made me do things to her. And then she made me have sex with her."

I was sure that Aazad was telling the truth because he was really upset, and I had never seen him upset about anything before. He was usually really happy. He told me that when it was over, she drove him half way back. Just far enough so he wouldn't be able to find her house again and cause any problems. He needed to walk the rest of the way back. And he said, "Before

I got out of her car, she told me if I ever tell anybody about it, she will tell the police that I broke into her house and raped her. She had kept evidence she said. And then I would go to jail for life or even be executed."

Of course I had heard lots of stories about street kids being bothered by men. That was the reason I always wanted to sleep near to somebody I knew. Because if I was sleeping alone at night, drunken men would sometimes start touching me. If I shouted they would usually walk away. Sometimes they would become aggressive and I would have to run for it. But I had never heard of anybody being bothered by a lady before.

◆ ◆ ◆

The story of Aazad reminds me of something that happened when I was collecting bottles to earn money because the *chai* boss was sick. I've never told this to anybody before. In fact I'd sort of forgotten about it for years. Or maybe I'd pushed it out of my head. I can do that sometimes with things I don't like to remember.

There was a man called Ramu-ji who I knew because he often came to drink *chai* when I worked at the *chai* stall. He had no wife, but he had a son of around my age who was usually with him. The boy didn't go to school. He had some kind of problem. He never looked at people and he almost never spoke, although I knew he could speak. I never knew what the boy was called. He stayed away from everybody, but he seemed OK with me because we were about the same age.

One day when I was out looking for empty bottles, I saw Ramu-ji and his son. Ramu-ji said they were just going to watch a video and he asked if I would like to go with them. So I said yes. They lived in a place quite close to the Jai Club, and they had a television and a DVD player. We watched cartoons for an hour, and then I went looking for more bottles. It was nice.

A few days later I saw Ramu-ji again, but his son wasn't

with him this time. He said they were going to watch more videos and asked if I would like to come to his home again. At that time, watching cartoons on a television was very special for me, and I was bored looking for bottles, so I said yes.

When we arrived at his place, his son wasn't there. So Ramu-ji said we should start to watch some videos until his son came home.

He sat very close to me and started to play a DVD. But this time it was hard-core pornography. I had never seen anything like that before. Then he grabbed hold of me with one arm and put his other hand inside my trousers and started touching me. I was so shocked I completely froze. He was a very respectable man, and I was always polite to him. I didn't know what to do or say, so I pulled myself free, and ran out of his house.

I always wondered if that was why his son seemed so depressed and never spoke to anybody. Because his father did things to him. Maybe the boy wasn't even his son. There was no mother. But I don't know if that was true. Of course I should have told somebody. Also to help the boy. But who would I tell? Who would believe the word of a street kid against a respectable man? So I never told anybody at all, before telling you now.

The strangest thing was, whenever I saw Ramu-ji after that day, it was as if he had completely forgotten about it, or it had never happened. He spoke to me just like he always did, and I was always polite back to him. But I never went near his house again.

I knew that sleeping away from papa could be dangerous. It made me look like an easy target, a young kid sleeping on his own in the street. But I was always lucky. Some other street kids had very bad stories about things that had happened to them.

Once a Swiss tourist who I had taken a few times in my rickshaw offered to pay me to have sex with him. He was even travelling with his wife and daughter at the time, but he'd left them behind at his hotel. He was very open about it. It was like he was asking me to drink a cup of *chai* with him. He said he would give me a lot of money for only one hour. I told him no, and that I didn't ever want to see him again. My friend Ajay, the high-caste street boy, was nearby, and he listened to what was going on. Ajay would do anything for money, and he offered himself to the Swiss man instead of me. But the man said Ajay was too old for him. He said he only liked the little ones.

But I don't want you to think all tourists were like that. Most foreigners were really nice to me.

Chapter 6: Kidnapped in Agra

My life settled into a kind of routine. I had grown a bit bigger, so I was getting more customers in my rickshaw. And when there was work at the marriage garden, I worked there instead. I got to know lots of people, and everybody in the neighbourhood knew who I was.

While I was working in the marriage garden, I became friendly with another boy who was a few years older than me. Everybody called him Agra-wallah, because he was always telling stories about Agra. I don't think anybody even knew what his real name was.

Agra-wallah was always saying things like, "I have a very big house in Agra. I have 2 sisters and I have motor cycle at my house in Agra." He had many, many stories about his life in Agra. Tall stories mainly. Everything was Agra, Agra, Agra. I never used to believe much of what he said because he also used to pull a rickshaw and do catering work at the marriage gardens. If he had a big house and a family and a motorbike in Agra as he said, then why would he be living alone, sleeping in the street in Jaipur? But he was a good guy. He was a good story-teller, and he always had something interesting to say. Like I said, I didn't believe much of it, but I was sure he had lived in Agra, because he really knew a lot about the city.

His stories made my life pulling a rickshaw and sleeping near to the Indiana Restaurant seem really boring. And it *was* boring. Doing the same things over and over. Always making just enough money to get by, but never enough to do anything interesting or even rent a room to sleep in.

I had never been anywhere outside of Jaipur besides Ajmer and Pushkar. Most of the people I knew had never been anywhere at all. They had never even left Jaipur. I was so curious about other places, and I wanted a chance to travel and see them. Although I had nearly drowned in Pushkar, it had been interesting to see somewhere new for a change.

Maybe that was what I liked about Agra-wallah. At least he had experienced more in his life than the M.I. Road. So I used to ask him lots of questions, and he liked that. I'd say, "Tell me more about the Red Fort in Agra. Is their *Mughlai* food spicier than food in Rajasthan? Is the Taj Mahal as beautiful as everybody says it is?" He used to say things like, "Yeah, the Taj is pretty nice. It's not far from my house." He enjoyed his role as a world traveller. And he often used to say, "I'm going to go and visit my family soon. Why don't you come along?"

Now that I didn't need to save for Raji's wedding, I started to think that maybe if I saved-up a bit of money, I could go to Agra with him one day and see the Taj Mahal.

Agra-wallah became a good friend and we hung around a lot together. He used to sleep in his rickshaw not so far from the Indiana. Sometimes I would park my rickshaw next to his so I could sleep in a safe place without hearing my papa shouting all night. If he wasn't there, I often used to sleep under the branches and roots of an old pipal tree, not so far away. I no longer had a regular place to sleep like most street people do.

One day I was drinking *chai* with Agra-wallah, and right out of the blue he said, "I'm going to visit my family in Agra on Sunday. I'll be staying for a few days. Why don't you come with me?" I told him I would think about it, and see if I had enough money saved. But he told me it wouldn't cost much. He said, "You don't need to worry. If you come with me, I'll take you to my house. I can show you Taj Mahal on my motorcycle. I have big family, and you can stay there, two days, three days ... as many days as you want to stay. You won't need to pay for food or anything, and I'll show you round the city."

I had some money saved, and it seemed like an exciting thing to do. Also, I had heard they had different food in Agra, and I wanted to try it. So I said, "Okay, I'll go with you on Sunday."

We made a plan to leave on Sunday at 5 o'clock. I took some of my savings, but I still had money saved with the security guard at the Indiana Restaurant. I locked my rickshaw on Sunday afternoon and met him at the bus station.

I told Agra-wallah that we should both buy our own tickets, but he asked if he could borrow the money for his ticket and he would pay me back when we were at his home in Agra. So I gave him the money to get two tickets. When the bus stopped for a break half way it was obvious that Agra-wallah had brought no money with him at all, because he asked me to pay for our food. Again he said he would pay me back later.

We reached Agra at around 1 a.m. the next morning, and when we got into a shared tuktuk, Agra-walla told the driver we were going to the train station. I was surprised and I asked him, "Why are we going to the train station? You told me your family lived close to the bus stand." But he said, "Everyone in my house will be sleeping by now. I don't want to disturb them by taking you there, and maybe they'll be angry with me too because I haven't been home for a long time. So we'll go in the morning. The bus station closes soon, but the train station is open all night. We can drink some *chai* there and rest a while. Then we'll go to my house for breakfast, when everybody is awake." He always had a way of making things sound reasonable.

So we hung around the train station all night. It seemed to me like Agra-walla was expecting to meet somebody there. He kept looking around. But if so, they didn't show up.

Then I saw somebody on the platform who I knew. It was a handicapped kid called Faraz, who used to beg sometimes outside Niro's Restaurant on the M.I. road in Jaipur. He had told me he lived in Agra, but when he was bored he used to come to beg from the tourists in Jaipur. I had spoken with him many times in Jaipur. He was a really good guy. I said, "Hi Faraz. Do you remember me from Jaipur?" He did. He said, "Hey, Naresh. What are you doing here in Agra?"

Although he was around my age, perhaps thirteen or

fourteen, he was really small and skinny, and he looked a lot younger than he was. He seemed even smaller because his legs were very thin and twisted, so he couldn't walk. His arms were also twisted and didn't work very well. He had been given a tricycle by the government that he could cycle with his hands, but that wasn't allowed in places like train stations, so he got around by sitting on a piece of wood with wheels under it, and pushing the ground with his hands. It was a bit like a skateboard, but not as cool. He also used to sit on that when he begged on the streets of Jaipur. He could go pretty fast on it too, but it looked really dangerous, because he was so low down that traffic couldn't see him.

I told him about coming to stay with Agra-wallah's family because I was bored with Jaipur and I wanted to see the Taj Mahal. Then he said, "I need to tell you something Naresh. Move your ear a bit closer so nobody else can hear." I sat down on the floor next to him. He said, "You need to be really careful. I know Agra-wallah. Nothing that he ever says is true. And he cheats everybody around him eventually. If you aren't careful, he'll cheat you too."

So I said, "Nooo, I've known him a long time. I know he makes up stories, but he's a good person really. He's a friend of mine. He won't cheat me."

Faraz said, "I hope you're right. But be careful. Don't turn your back on him. And watch out for the kids that hang around the station here. I know them all and you can't trust any of them."

He told me he came to Agra train station most evenings to beg from rich tourists who got off the night train from Delhi, but he was tired now and so he was going home. He lived in a room not far from the station. So he said goodbye, and then he scooted away on his skateboard, weaving in between people's legs, and he was gone.

Faraz was a really nice boy, and I knew he was an honest person. People beg for different reasons. Some are really not poor, they beg because they make lots of money begging and they can't be bothered to work. Some beg because they have no other way to survive at the moment. I know how that feels. It's horrible. A lot of street kids need to beg. For them begging is better than stealing. But people like Faraz are different. He couldn't read or write, and he couldn't walk or use his hands, so what choice did he have? How could he ever have a job? I knew he was really intelligent, and I should have listened to him, but I was so excited about being in a new city for the first time, that I ignored his advice.

Then, at around 5 a.m., Agra-wallah suddenly announced it was time to go back to the bus station. "But why?" I asked him. "That's where we came from a few hours ago. Why don't we go to your house?" As usual he made it all sound reasonable. He said the bus station would be open by now. We could drink some more *chai* there, and then a bit later we could take a local bus to his house. So again, I paid for the shared tuktuk back to the bus stand. It had all seemed like a big waste of time and money to me. It really felt like he'd been waiting for somebody at the train station who didn't show up.

While we were drinking *chai* at the bus station, Agra-wallah said, "Naresh, I need to tell you something ... I haven't been home in a long time, so I was thinking that maybe I should buy something for my family members." So I asked, "What can you get here in a bus station?" He said, "Yeah, nothing very good. But I don't want to disappoint them. So maybe I could take some *peda* and a box of *mithaiyan*. There's a shop just outside the station." He said if I went to buy two local bus tickets, he would go and buy the biscuits and box of sweets, and he would meet me at the bus stop in ten minutes. Oh ... but wait a minute ... he didn't have any money, so could I also lend him a bit more. I had enough change to buy the two bus tickets, but I only had a five hundred rupee note left. So I loaned that to him. I told him it was the last of my money, so I needed him to give the change back to me.

Our bus left, and there was no sign of Agra-wallah. When I had waited for an hour at the bus stop, I felt pretty sure that he had run off with what was left of my money. And after three hours, I was completely sure about it. I tried to get my money back for the bus tickets, but they told me they had already been clipped, so there were no refunds. And when I tried to get on the bus back to Jaipur, I found out that Agra-wallah had also used my money to buy single tickets from Jaipur to Agra, not the returns that I had paid for. I couldn't read what was on the tickets so I didn't know that until the bus driver stopped me getting on.

I sat down on a bench to think for a while. I was in a strange city, I had almost no money left, and I had no way to get back to Jaipur except maybe by walking. That might take me two weeks, and by then I would have starved to death. The only option seemed to be to ride the train back without a ticket.

I had less than twenty rupees left. Then I thought about Faraz, the handicapped boy. He said he visited the train station most evenings, and he lived nearby. I thought, he's such a nice guy, I'm sure he'll help me. Perhaps he'll lend me the money for a ticket. At least he could show me which was the train to Jaipur and then I could sit in the toilet without a ticket. The train station was much too far to walk, so I decided to spend the last of my money on a shared tuktuk.

As soon as I arrived I searched the station for Faraz. I walked up and down the platforms, but he was nowhere to be found. I was really hungry, because I hadn't eaten anything the entire day, but my money was finished.

I saw a big group of maybe fifteen street kids who were begging on trains and hanging around the station, and I asked if they knew Faraz. They shook their heads. So I said, "You must know him. He's a handicapped kid. A Muslim. Really small and thin. He was here last night."

Then of them said, "Oh yeah, that little guy on the wheels. He comes here every evening. But it's too early for him now. He always comes just before the Delhi train arrives." Then a train pulled in and all the kids jumped on board to beg from the passengers or pretend to clean the floor for tips. A few minutes later they were back. They had a big bag of food with them, and they sat on the platform to eat together. One of them saw me watching and called me over.

You may think street kids are all the same. They aren't. I knew kids like these, and I was afraid of them. I knew they were only doing what they needed to survive. But some of the boys were bigger and much stronger than me. I'd known plenty of boys like them. They always had a gang and they kept their power by bullying the weaker ones in the gang. It's the same way that many rich people keep their money and power. Also, I had seen the kids sniffing glue in plastic bags earlier, and I'd noticed they all had cuts and scars on their faces and arms. Perhaps they did that to themselves, or maybe it was from fighting, I wasn't sure. I'd seen many groups of kids like them on trains.

I knew that if I got involved with them I'd be pulled into their world of crime and drugs and trouble. Everything I sensed told me to stay away from them, but also to stay friendly with them. So even though I was really hungry, I smiled and told them I'd already eaten too much.

Another train pulled in and they all ran to get on it. They left their bag of food behind on the platform. I could see a pile of fries and other things. I was so hungry, I got up to go and steal some of it. But then they got off the train again, so I pretended I was just going to get a drink of water.

I sat there for hours, trying not to cry, waiting for Faraz to arrive. But he never came.

Then a man came over to me. He said, "I've been watching you for a long time sitting there little boy. Why are you crying?" I didn't know what to say. I told him I wasn't really crying for a reason.

He took a plastic card out of his pocket, and he said, "This is my ID. I help children who get lost or separated from their family while they are travelling. I work on behalf of a charity." He showed me his card again and said, "Look this is the name of the charity." The card had a photo of him and some writing that was probably his name and the name of the organization he worked for. Then he sat down beside me, and said, "I can help you. But you need to tell me the truth about what has happened." So I told him everything. How my friend had brought me to Agra, and how he had cheated me out of all my money and disappeared. And besides that, I was really hungry because I hadn't eaten anything since last night.

He was very friendly, and he said, "Don't worry, I'll make sure you reach Jaipur tomorrow. There's no train there tonight, but I can take you to an ashram where lots of kids stay. I live there myself. You can eat something, get a good night's sleep, and we'll solve all your problems tomorrow."

So I walked with him to his ashram. The kids from the platform followed behind us at a distance as well. They all knew him, and they were very careful how they spoke to him, calling him master-ji. Then I realised that they also probably lived in the place where he was taking me. But I thought, it doesn't matter, he can take me anywhere. I just want to eat some food, and sleep, and I'll leave in the morning. If he was lying about getting me to Jaipur, I'd go back to the train station and travel back without a ticket.

When we reached the ashram, the man rang a bell and the group of street kids from the station followed us inside. We walked through a high metal gate into a compound, and then I became worried, because there was a man waiting who locked the gate behind us with a big padlock and a heavy chain. Even worse, there was a building in the compound, and I could see that all the windows had shutters that were locked with heavy chains.

I was taken into an office where another man was sitting. He took out a pen and opened a book to write in. He said, "What's your name and your date of birth?" So I told him my name was

Naresh, but of course, I didn't know my date of birth, I didn't even know how old I was in years. So I told him I didn't know my date of birth. Then he said, "I need your *full* name. What's your family name?"

Perhaps you remember I told you back at the start of this whole story that some street kids don't know their real name? If you thought I was exaggerating, then this is going to shock you, because there was something I didn't tell you then. I didn't know what my own surname was. I was just called Naresh. I'd never needed a surname before. I had never been to school, or been registered anywhere. And my papa had never told me what our family name was.

I said, "Sir, I don't know any other name. I'm just called Naresh. Nobody has ever asked me for my surname. People only ever ask me what my caste is." Perhaps he thought I was pretending, to hide something. Maybe he thought I was a complete idiot who didn't even know his own name. But it was the truth. I felt really stupid. So he said, "Well, what caste are you then?" I told him I was Sindhi. So he wrote down 'Naresh Sindhi.' I know that because he said it out loud while he was writing.

Then he said he would contact my parents, so what were their names and their address and phone number. I told him my papa was called Tikam Das, but of course I didn't know his surname. And I said he didn't have a telephone or even an address. He slept on the pavement in Jaipur, near to the Indiana Restaurant in C-scheme. How could I expect him to contact my papa? There was no way to do it, and I couldn't even tell him my papa's full name.

Then he said, "Empty your pockets and bags onto the table." I was carrying two plastic bags. One of them belonged to Agra-wallah. He had left it behind when he ran off with my money. There was nothing interesting or valuable in either of them. I asked why he wanted to look in my bags, and he said most of the children here were drug users, so their bags and pockets were always checked on the way in.

It didn't seem like an ashram to me. The man in the office was clearly a Muslim, and ashrams are always Hindu. So I asked what kind of ashram it was. He said, "This isn't an ashram, it's an orphanage." That made me even more worried. But I thought, no matter what happens, I'll leave tomorrow when the kids from the station leave.

Then he said, "Go and sit on the floor." I said "OK. But sir, I am feeling very hungry. Can I have some food to eat please?" He told me the food wasn't ready yet. The cook was late. And everybody would get food at about 10:30 or 11 o'clock. By then I was starting to feel dizzy because I had no energy left.

The room was full of little kids lying on the floor wrapped in blankets. Twenty or more of them, boys and girls. Some were just eight or nine years old, others were teenagers, up to about seventeen. They were all really quiet, but the other kids from the station sat together in a corner talking and making a lot of noise. I was shown where I could take some blankets from a pile.

I lay down on one blanket, pulled another one over my head, and started crying. It had not been a good couple of days.

Around midnight, everybody was woken up and told that the food was ready. The station kids were already sitting waiting.

I may have been just a street kid, but I knew what good food was, and this was *really* bad. It certainly wasn't the special *Mughlai* food that Agra was famous for. I was given some *tari* with a single piece of meat in it and one chapatti. I couldn't even tell what kind of meat it was. Since the place was run by Muslims, I knew that at least it wouldn't be pig. It could have been mutton, but it was really tough, so maybe it was even buffalo.

The chapatti was really thin and I ate it in one go because I was very hungry. I thought I'd get a few more because it's normal to eat several chapattis with your dinner. As soon as I had finished it, I asked, "Sir, may I have another chapatti please?" But he said, "Everybody here gets only one chapatti." So I said, "But sir, I'm very hungry. I haven't eaten anything since yesterday." He just said, "We don't have any more. They're finished. Here everyone gets only one chapatti." As soon as I had chewed and swallowed the piece of buffalo, they set me to work washing the dishes.

When I lay down to sleep I thought, I'll leave this place in the morning. The man who brought me here will come to pick me up. And if he doesn't, it won't matter, I'll leave anyway.

I hardly slept at all that night, even though I was really tired, but finally it was morning. I got up and washed my face. Then I asked, "Sir, when will I go?" The man from the office said, "The man who dropped you here will come to pick you up in a while." So I said, "Okay." That sounded fine.

They gave me some *chai* to drink. And at about 10 a.m., they gave me a little bowl of breakfast *poha*, which is steamed and flattened rice. When it's mixed with vegetables and sauce, poha can be great. But on its own it's dry and really boring. It tastes of nothing much, just cold rice. Breakfast was dry poha. But I ate it quickly and asked, "Sir, may I have some more please? I'm really hungry." He got angry again and said, "No. You only get that amount here. Don't keep asking for more again and again. You'll eat what we give you. Everyone here is happy with that. And you should be too."

After we had been given the *poha*, the kids from the station were allowed to leave the room and the door was locked behind them. Then the gate outside was unlocked so they could go. But most of them came back to sleep in the evening. Nobody else was allowed to leave. None of the other kids seemed to care about it.

While I was waiting, I looked around the building to see if there was a way to escape. All the windows were locked with thick chains. It looked nothing like an ashram, it looked like a children's prison. I tried speaking with some of the kids, but it was like they were drugged or something. They were not interested in anything and could hardly be bothered to speak. I asked how long they had been here. For some, it was three years, others four years. Most didn't remember how long, it was just years. They were all dirty and they only had one set of clothes, so they were filthy too. I went upstairs and looked through a crack in a window shutter. I could see there was a yard and a big gate that was locked with chains.

After two days, I was getting desperate. When I was speaking to the man in the office, I started crying. I said, "Sir, please let me go, if I have done anything wrong then please forgive me. I just want to go home." He said, "We can't let you go. We have responsibilities. If you want to cry, then cry. It won't make any difference. You'll need to be patient and wait. When he has time, the man who brought you here will take you to the station and will put you on a train."

The only thing that happened that day was the food was different. Potato curry with one chapatti. It was about the worst curry I had ever tasted in my life.

The next morning I asked again, "Sir, has he come yet?" But the man in the office said, "He'll come when he has time. You need to be patient." So I said, "If he's not coming or he's busy, then please open the door and I'll leave. I'll go to the station and sleep there tonight, and get the train back to Jaipur tomorrow morning." But he said, "No, no, we can't just let you go. You need to be patient and stop asking all the time. We'll tell you when he comes." But by night, he still hadn't come.

The next day I asked time and again. Each time I was told the man was very busy at another ashram, or he didn't answer his phone, or he will definitely come tomorrow. And I asked over and over to be allowed to leave, but I was told the same story, that I needed to wait, because the man would come soon to put me on the train to Jaipur.

◆ ◆ ◆

By then I had learned that the orphanage was run as a

charity. They called it an NGO. It wasn't a proper government orphanage. It was paid for by donations from rich people. I don't imagine any of the rich people had ever visited it. Otherwise they would have seen that not much of their money was spent looking after the kids. It was run by two men who also lived in the building. They were both quite young, around thirty or so. One was very muscled. He did the cooking. The other wore glasses and looked like a school teacher. He worked in the office. Perhaps they were brothers, or just friends. They lived somewhere in a private area upstairs.

There were two big rooms, each of around 50 square metres. About twenty or twenty-five kids slept there on the stone floor, with boys and girls sleeping in the same room. All the girls were very young. There were no older girls. They were all very thin and sick-looking because they never went outside and they were given so little food. There was dirt everywhere and the walls were greasy yellow. Each night the kids would take a dirty old blanket from a pile so they could sleep on the concrete floor. Everybody had to fold their blanket and put it back on the pile in the morning. Some of the kids kept a towel wrapped around them all day because their clothes were so badly torn underneath it. Most of the kids who had been there a long time would sit around the whole day without speaking. There was no school, or anything for them to do. Some of them used to scratch and cut themselves because they were so bored.

There was one toilet, but the door was broken so you could easily see when somebody was using it, and there was one shower with only cold water and no door at all. When a kid wanted to take a shower, another had to hold a blanket across the door so nobody could see.

The kids from the train station only slept there each night. They were allowed to leave in the morning to go and sniff glue at the station. The orphanage owners knew they would return in the evening because they had nowhere else to sleep. They ate food during the day, so they didn't care about getting only one chapatti with some stewed buffalo or something at night. On the way in, their bags and pockets were checked for knives and drugs, and maybe for any money. But I don't think they would have been so stupid to have money in their pockets.

I also knew why the other kids were kept there as prisoners. Because you can't earn money from a private orphanage if there are no orphans. They were trapped there so the rich people would continue to donate money.

I started to feel very worried. I realised that a lot of those lost kids who had been stuck there for years were there because they didn't officially exist. Just like me. They had nowhere to go and nobody to go to. Or they had someone, but no way to contact them, so nobody could come to get them. Their families would think they had disappeared. The world had told them they didn't matter, and they had started to believe it, so they just stayed there and asked no questions. However bad things may have been over the years for me, I realized I was really fortunate. I did matter to people. I was lucky because I had my papa and my sister. And I had some good friends in Jaipur who cared about me. But I also knew that unless I made a serious effort to get out of there, I could be stuck in that children's jail for years. I would be there until one day they decided that I wasn't a child anymore, and opened the door so I could go outside and sleep on the streets of Agra instead.

Sitting there thinking, hour after hour, day after day, I thought, perhaps by the time I got out, my papa would be dead, from drinking a bad bottle of *kachchi daru*, or maybe from a fight in the street one night when he was drunk. By then, perhaps Raji might have moved house, maybe to another city, and I would never be able to find her again. Then I would also have nowhere to go, and nobody to go to. All these kinds of thoughts were going through my head. I knew that however my papa might have behaved lately, he loved me. His addiction changed him, and he was addicted because there had been so much bad luck in his life. It was the drink, not him, that did it. Underneath the alcohol he was the same papa who used to cycle around the city with Raji and me sitting on a big soft bag of cloth on the back of his rickshaw, in the days when we were happy together, and he was always funny and kind. Even when he was hardly able to walk, he had once jumped out of a moving train for me. And I realized how much I loved him too, and I felt really sorry that I had stayed away from him for so long instead of trying to help him.

◆ ◆ ◆

Quickly, I didn't know what day it was. All the days were the same. Nothing happened. Then a new boy arrived. He looked confused as they brought him inside and locked the door behind him. Within about ten minutes he had stopped being confused and had already started to be angry.

His name was Jishnu. He threw a couple of dusty blankets on the floor near to me and sat down. "What is this place?" he asked me. "A fucking prison? These blankets stink. Do they seriously expect me to sleep like this on the floor?"

He was right. The blankets were all full of lice, and they smelled very bad. It didn't matter to me, nor was it new to me, because I had slept under a much smellier blanket when I used to work at the *chai* stall. When our clothes and mattresses got wet during the rainy season they smelled even worse.

Jishnu was very different from the other kids. He was expensively dressed and educated. A smart kid, a few years older than me. And so a street kid and a rich kid became friends immediately because we could both see we had something in common. We were both determined to get out of that place. There were clearly three groups of kids. The glue-sniffers from the station who were making noise and messing around in one corner, the other kids who had all given up and sat around doing nothing, and us, me and Jishnu.

Jishnu told me he had been travelling from Jodhpur to his

home in Bihar. When he realised he had taken a wrong train, he had got off at Agra station. While he was trying to figure out how to get from Agra to Bihar, he had met the child catcher, who had told him the same story, that tomorrow he would be put on a train home after he had spent the night at an ashram. He looked worried when I said I had been told that same story many days ago, but the man had never returned and they wouldn't let me go. And anyway, it wasn't an ashram, it was some kind of private orphanage. I had also heard that the child catcher got paid for each lost kid he brought there, and that the kids from the station helped him find new kids.

Of course Jishnu knew his name and address, but he didn't know his father's telephone number. He'd lost the piece of paper it was written on. Such a rich boy would have a mobile phone today, but in those days not even many adults had one.

The next morning, when Jishnu was not put on a train as they had promised him, he became so angry he was almost crying. "They say they're going to write a letter to my father. A letter! That could take a week to even arrive. Who do those *madarchod* – mother-fuckers – think they are? I'm not an orphan and I'm not staying here like some fucking prisoner sleeping in the dirt and eating that shit food. My father is a rich and powerful man. They'd better be careful when he finds out about this."

So more than once a day, Jishnu would go and annoy the man in the office. I would hear him shouting and swearing. *Madarchod* is about the worst swear-word you can use in Hindi. I had never heard a kid call an adult that before. But they knew they needed to be careful how they treated Jishnu, because they couldn't keep a rich kid, and his family might be dangerous. I think the child catcher had made a big mistake bringing him. Perhaps Jishnu's father really was a rich gangster who would send people to beat them up, like he told them.

Jishnu made me feel more confident, so I also started to annoy the man in the office, but I knew I needed to be more clever about it because I was not a rich kid. I had to be polite and be sure I didn't make him too angry. On the other hand, I had to let him see that I would never ever stop until he let me out. Like I told you, I can be very stubborn. I may not have been to school, but I was no idiot, and he needed to see that. So I would say calmly and politely, "*Bade bhai*, this is an orphanage, but I am not an orphan. I have a father in Jaipur and a sister and a *bua* in Ajmer. I would like to go home please." Then the next time, "*Bhai sahib*, you are not allowed to keep me here. There are laws against it. I am not a prisoner. I want to go back to my papa in Jaipur please." And as Jishnu became a bigger and bigger problem for them, calling them lying mother-fuckers and shouting about how his father would send people to kill them when he found out they were keeping him as a prisoner, I got more confident. I said, "The family of my sister's husband are rich. When I send a message to them, I'll ask them to find a lawyer and bring the police. You have kidnapped me and that's against the law." They could see that Jishnu and I had become good friends. And they knew they could never keep him, so perhaps I did have a way to get a message out. And I thought if we both make problems for them they might let us both go to end the problems.

I was totally sure they would send that letter to Jishnu's father as they said they would, but he didn't trust them. And he decided he wasn't going to wait around to find out. He told me he had noticed a window that would be easy to break open. When everything was quiet, we checked it out. He was right. It wasn't as well locked as the rest. It could probably be forced open by the two of us working together. So we started to make plans. As I sat there thinking it over and over, it became like a Bollywood movie in my head. In the afternoon when everybody was busy, we would sneak upstairs and break the lock on the window. Then we would both jump out into the street. Jishnu would hurt his ankle when he landed, but I would help him, and we would walk together to the train station, keeping away from the main roads, because, by then, they would be following us and would have told the police that we had broken out. At the train station, I would find my train to Jaipur and he would find his train back home to Bihar. Just as the police arrived at the station, we would say goodbye on the platform, like two Bollywood heroes, and jump on our trains to escape. I would have no ticket, but I would sit near to the train door, and if the TTE came along, I would jump out of the train like my papa had done that time.

◆ ◆ ◆

In those days, because I couldn't read or write, I had to keep everything stored in my head. That made me have an amazing memory for details. I still do. Sometimes it's like I have a photograph stored in my mind.

Sitting on the floor of that prison, hour after hour, day in day out, thinking, I suddenly realized that I did know a phone number. Just one. There was a barber close to the Jai club. He was not the kind of barber you would recognize. His barber's chair was underneath a tree in the street, and he had a little mirror pinned to the tree trunk. He had worked there in the street for years. He was called Bunty, and I knew him very well. He was a good, honest person. He had a mobile phone, and he had once given me a piece of paper with his number on it. The number was not for me, because I didn't have a phone then. It was in case any of my rickshaw customers ever wanted to get a haircut. I also used to give it to my foreign customers so they could phone it if they ever needed a rickshaw and Bunty could tell me. But nobody ever phoned it for me. I couldn't read words, but I did know how to read numbers. I had read Bunty's phone number a few times, and I realized it was still in my head. I could remember it … almost. I wasn't sure if the last two numbers were 85 or 58, but I was sure about the rest of it. So I had two possible numbers in my memory, one of which I was sure was Bunty's.

This time when I went to annoy the man in the office, I told him I had remembered the telephone number of a family friend. I asked him to dial the 58 number. I think he agreed to keep me quiet. But that number didn't ring. Then I asked him to try the 85 number instead. He let me see he was annoyed, but he dialled it to finally shut me up. Then Bunty answered. I could hear his voice from across the desk and I started to cry. I could hear him saying, "Yes, I know Naresh very well" and "Yes, I also know his father, Tikam Das. He sleeps near to the Jai club."

I asked Bunty if he would collect all the money I had saved from the security guard at the Indiana Restaurant and come to Agra to rescue me as soon as possible. But he needed to be careful that he didn't tell papa. If papa knew I had some money saved, it would all get spent on his alcohol addiction and I would still be stuck here. I wondered if papa had even noticed that I was missing. Perhaps he thought I was only staying away from him because I was still angry about Raji's wedding.

They told Bunty that he would need to bring some ID to collect me, and they gave him an address in Agra where he could wait for me. Bunty said he couldn't come tomorrow, but he would take an overnight train and collect me the day after.

When it was arranged, and Bunty was on the way, like Jishnu, I didn't need to be so careful with the man in the office anymore. And I was very angry by then. I said to him, "You're a liar! You lied to me over and over about the man coming to put me on a train. Why?" But he just said, "We have responsibilities. We can't simply let children go."

I told Jishnu that I was going to get out, and I promised him that I would contact his father immediately and tell him everything. But I didn't need to. There was a phone call and Jishnu was called into the office. He returned with a big grin on his face and said, "Ha, that lying sister-fucker is really scared now. My father told him he will be in serious trouble if I've been mistreated. And if I've been hurt, he'll get hurt much worse."

Actually, to be fair, I never saw any violence at the orphanage. Nobody ever got hit, and the two guys only ever shouted if there was too much noise. Nobody really seemed to be afraid of them. Nobody seemed to care much about anything. They had all given up, so they never caused any problems.

◆ ◆ ◆

So Jishnu and I were taken to a photographer's shop. We were photographed and then we were dropped at a police office in Agra train station. Jishnu was given a ticket and put on a train to Bihar. I think the man in the office really did not want to meet his father.

When Bunty arrived I started crying. He said, "It's OK, don't worry. I'm here to take you home." Then a policeman took all the details from Bunty. He looked at the form from the orphanage and he asked me, "What's your surname and your age?" I said "I don't know my surname. I don't have any documents. I don't remember anything." So he said, "It's OK, then it stays 'Naresh Sindhi.' I'll write that you are thirteen." They took more photos of me, and then together with Bunty and the policeman, and I was allowed to go.

When we left the police office, Bunty asked, "Did you visit the Taj Mahal while you were here?" I told him I hadn't. He said, "Shall we go and take a look at it now before we leave?" I knew he was only joking, but I told him I never ever wanted to see the Taj Mahal, and I never ever wanted to come back to Agra in my whole life. I wanted to go home to Jaipur and stay there.

◆ ◆ ◆

I had never seen my papa cry before. But he cried a lot when I arrived home. I think we had both learned how much we meant to one another, and how easily we could lose one another. And I had never before felt so happy to sleep in the street outside the Jai Club. The next morning, I asked my papa what our family name is. It's Kishwani.

◆ ◆ ◆

For several days when I was back in Jaipur I was really depressed. I couldn't believe that a friend would have deceived me and treated me like that. And I couldn't get that children's prison out of my head. I knew I could easily have still been there, trapped for years, like all those other poor lost kids who have nobody to listen to them.

Soon, word started to get around among the rickshaw pullers about how I'd been snatched by a child catcher and thrown into an orphanage. Some took it seriously, but others made fun of me. So when people asked about it, I started to tell the Bollywood version, in which I had been kidnapped and made to work, but I'd escaped by jumping out of a window. But then I told everybody that none of the stories were true. I had made them all up for fun. I had only been away visiting my *bua* in Ajmer.

◆ ◆ ◆

Some while later, I saw Agra-wallah walking on the M.I. road. It was the first time I had seen him since he had run off with all my money at the bus station in Agra. I was shocked, and I stopped and looked at him. He stopped too and smiled. Then he stuck his chin out in the kind of way that means, 'So, what a you going to do about it, loser?' Instantly, I was so angry I wanted to go and smash him in the face. I wanted to kick him and punch him and really hurt him. But I didn't. I just stood there looking at him without showing any emotions. He continued smiling and then walked away. I never saw him again after that day.

I guess Agra-wallah thought he had won. He had played a clever game for months pretending to be my friend so he could cheat me out of a little bit of money. Maybe he thought it was worth all that effort to steal five hundred rupees. That's about six or seven US dollars. And he thought he had got away with it too. But maybe, one day, he'll read this book, and realise that he didn't.

Chapter 7: From downward to upward

After I returned from Agra, my life went back to the normal routine. I started sleeping near to my papa again. He still drank a lot, but maybe he had learned something. He still got noisy and shouted at night, but it was never as bad as before. Or maybe I had become more tolerant of him. He never tried to hit me again, no matter how much he drank or how angry he became.

Tourists became my specialty because my English was getting better by the day and I was more confident. My regular spot to pick up tourists was now outside McDonalds at *Panch Batti* junction on the M.I. Road. That was where lots of tourists could be found during the daytime.

Besides tourists, lots of call girls used to hang around near McDonalds because they used the public restroom that was nearby. Some would come three or four times a day. Many had their own tuktuk driver who always worked with them, taking them to and from clients. But some would take any rickshaw or tuktuk that was available. After using the public toilet or having a shower, they would take one of the rickshaws waiting outside McDonalds to go to their next client.

One of the call girls was called Kali, like the name of the really dangerous goddess. But it wasn't her real name. Nobody knew what that was. Kali had very dark skin, just like the goddess. Perhaps her family was from South India. She was about twenty years of age and she was very friendly, and prettier than most of the others were. She used to talk with everybody and she smiled a lot. Kali often wanted to sit in my rickshaw because I had a music system in the back for my clients. She was a funny person, but I always told her that I was waiting for a client who was eating. She knew it wasn't true, but she would deliberately do it as a joke to tease me. I liked Kali, and I had nothing against any of the other call girls, but I knew they were always surrounded by trouble. I had heard lots of stories from other rickshaw pullers. There were always problems with clients or pimps, with fights and arguments and things like that.

When I was still working at the *chai* stall I overheard lots of things. I once heard a customer telling a story about how he had gone with a call girl in a rickshaw. She had asked for one thousand rupees. He needed to pay eight hundred in advance, and the rest when it was over. On the way to her room she had told him that she had to pick up her keys, so they needed to stop for a minute. Then she disappeared down a side street with his eight hundred rupees. The rickshaw driver was left with an angry client who wouldn't pay him for the ride.

I'd heard many other stories. Some much worse. So I would never take call girls as passengers. But one night Kali suddenly appeared from nowhere and sat in my rickshaw while I was talking with some other rickshaw pullers. When I asked her to get out, she said, "Today I want to hear no bullshit from you young man. I need to go home, and you are going to drop me there." As usual, I said "I can't. I have clients eating in McDonald's. And anyway, you know I don't take local passengers, I only take tourists." So she said, "Yeah, yeah, I've heard all this crap over and over from you. But I'm tired and I need to go home. So get moving." She wouldn't get out of the rickshaw, and one of the tuktuk drivers said to me, "What are you afraid of? Cycle her home. Nothing's going to happen!"

So I started to cycle her in the direction of her home. Jaipur doesn't have a red light area like most cities do. I know there's an area close to the airport where everything is available. I've never been there, but from what I hear it sounds like a really dangerous place.

When we were near Statue Circle, Kali turned my music system on very loud and wouldn't turn it down. She was like a naughty child with too much energy, always behaving badly. It was night time, so that attracted a lot of attention. And she kept leaning forward and shouting things to me over the music. I don't like to attract attention, so it made me uncomfortable.

After a kilometre or so, two men on motorbikes pulled level with us and then made me stop. They asked Kali to go with them. But she refused. She said she was tired and wanted to go home. She said she would see them another time. One of them said, "All the girls go with us except you. What's the problem? Are you too good for us?"

Kali told me to cycle away, but they kept following us. Then they pulled alongside us again. One of them was waving a big knife. He shouted to Kali, "You better come with us, otherwise you won't make it home in once piece." I became really scared. They were angry and they seemed to be serious. Kali also seemed scared, and I don't think many things scared her.

There was a police station close by, and Kali shouted so that the men could hear her that we should go there. She said she knew all of the policemen there. That was probably true. All the call girls paid some policemen to look after them, or to look away when they were breaking the law. I had heard of men being made to give all their money and their mobile phone to a policeman who worked with a call girl, rather than have their family find out what they had been doing.

I cycled Kali towards the police station, but the two men kept following us, with that crazy guy waving his big *rampuri* dagger, sometimes at Kali and sometimes at me. I was really scared. This was exactly why I never took any of the call girls as passengers.

The police station had a yard at the front and I cycled into that, but the men stayed outside the gate. As Kali had said, the policemen all knew her, and a couple of them walked out to the street to take a look. Of course the men had gone by then.

While Kali was talking to the policemen, telling them what had happened, two other men on motorcycles drove up the street and stopped near to the gate. One of the cops said, "Are those the guys that were following you?" And Kali said yes they were. I tried to tell her that they were different guys, but the police had already grabbed hold of them. One policeman blew a whistle and suddenly a few cops ran out of the station with *lathi* sticks and started beating the men. They were dragged into the police station. One of them was shouting, "What have we done? What have we done?" And one of the cops said, "You were molesting this young girl."

I tried to tell them that they had the wrong guys, but there was a lot of noise and shouting, and nobody was interested in listening to some rickshaw boy. Kali followed them inside, but I thought, 'This has nothing to do with me. I need to get away.'

Then one of the policemen, a very big and heavy one, said to me, "So you're a rickshaw driver for prostitutes are you?" He knew I wasn't. The permanent drivers for call girls were always big tough guys who drove tuktuks. They all had scars on their faces from getting into fights. One had an eye missing that had been poked out in argument with somebody. None of the call girls had a young kid cycling them around.

So I said, "No. I was just waiting at McDonalds and she got into my rickshaw." He said, "Yeah sure! You can come inside the station as well." I told him, "Sir, I didn't do anything. I'm just a rickshaw driver." Then he slapped me so hard across the side of my head that I could hear a whistling noise in my left ear for days afterwards. I was still just a young kid and I started crying. He said, "Park your rickshaw outside in the street, and get back in here immediately." So I walked my rickshaw through the gate and out into the street. I glanced back and saw that the cop was going inside. After my experience in Agra, I was really terrified. There was no way I was going into a police station. So I jumped on my rickshaw and started to cycle faster and faster and faster. I was shaking with fear. I cycled at full speed through the streets without stopping for anything. I didn't even look behind until I had reached the Indiana Restaurant. But luckily nobody had followed me.

When I sat down to catch my breath, it brought everything back into my mind about being locked in that kids' prison in Agra. And I thought, if they had locked me up at the police station, who would have come to get me out this time?

It was a good lesson. I made sure I never again took a call girl as a passenger in my rickshaw. I saw Kali often after that night, but she never again asked me to take her anywhere. She was a good person and she knew she could have caused big problems for me.

◆ ◆ ◆

One evening when I was on my way home to sleep I saw two men coming out of the Indiana Restaurant. One was Indian and the other was a foreigner with a big white beard. If he had been sitting on the back of a fish, he might have looked like *Jhulelal*, the god of the Sindhi people. I asked them if they needed a rickshaw and they said yes. They wanted to go to an expensive hotel. But then they looked me up and down and said, "No, no. You're really young and we're very heavy. You won't be able to manage us. So I said, as I always did, "I can do it. I'm very strong. I can get you safely to your hotel."

While I was saying that, a tuktuk pulled up and the driver started telling them how I was too young and would cause an accident, and how they should go with him instead. The Western man with the white beard – he was Spanish I later learned – got annoyed with the pushy tuktuk driver. So he sat down in my rickshaw and said, "No, we'll go with the young boy. He says he can do it, and I believe him."

When I dropped them at their hotel, they asked how much it cost. Most people wanted to agree to a price before you set off because they thought you would cheat them later by asking for too much. I knew some rickshaw pullers did that. But I said, "Thirty rupees please." The Western man said, "Only thirty? We paid five hundred for a taxi to get to the restaurant." So the Indian man gave me thirty rupees and then the Western man handed me five hundred. I said to him, "No sir, the trip is only thirty rupees." He didn't seem to speak very good English, but he said something quickly in Spanish to the Indian man. He told me in Hindi that it was a tip and I should keep it. I told you about that one time a client had paid me five hundred for the ride to his hotel, but nobody had ever given me such a big tip before.

Then the Spanish man asked me a few things and his friend translated into Hindi and translated my answers into Spanish. He asked, "Do you go to school?" I told him I had never been to school. Then he asked, "Where do you live?" So I told him I slept in the street in front of the Indiana Restaurant, and I had been on my way home to sleep when I met them. He looked shocked. He told me they would eat again at the Indiana the next evening. They would eat quite late after they had finished working. I should bring them to their hotel tomorrow as well.

The next evening I asked the security guard at the Indiana if he had seen them go in, an Indian man and a tall foreign man with a big white beard. They looked like businessmen. The security guard saw everything and he told me they were inside. He said they had been coming each evening for a few days and always left very late at about 11 or 12. So I waited for them.

When they came out I dropped them at their hotel and asked for thirty rupees again. This time the Spanish man offered me one thousand rupees tip. Nothing like that had ever happened before. It would take me weeks to earn that much. I was confused, and I was a bit suspicious as well. So I said, "No sir, I will take only the thirty rupees."

The Spanish man smiled and said, "That's very honest of you young man, but don't worry, I'm very rich." I still refused the money, but he pushed the thousand rupees into my shirt pocket. He said, "We'll be back again tomorrow. I hope you can pick us up." And then they went into their hotel. They behaved like the money was nothing to them.

It was funny, because the Spanish man was very rich, but he didn't speak very good English. All other rich tourists I had met spoke better English than me, but his English was not much better than my level. When I was trying to get to sleep later, I kept thinking about it and I felt worried. I thought, maybe they are trying to lure me somewhere with all that money. Nobody gives you money for nothing. There must be a reason. And I thought, 'I need to be really careful. Maybe they have something bad in mind.' Some of the rickshaw drivers told stories of how Western people would kidnap you to sell your organs. Then you would be found dead somewhere with your heart and liver missing. I didn't believe any of those stupid stories. The rickshaw drivers were just afraid of foreigners. But still I was getting a bit worried.

On the third night they came out of the Indiana and I dropped them at their expensive hotel. And the Spanish man started asking questions again, which his friend translated into Hindi for me. He asked me, "Why don't you go to school?" I said, "I have no other option. I wasn't sent to school as a little kid, and now I'm too old to start, because I can't read or write." Then he said, "If I arrange a school for you, will you go?" I was confused, but I said I would. Of course I knew I couldn't really. If I went to school there would be no money. Then who would support me? Not my papa.

The Indian man told me the Spanish man was his boss. He said he was a very rich businessman who owned a big tourist company. And he said if I studied well, the Spanish man could arrange for me to go and live in Spain. He said his boss had been talking about how he might even adopt me because he didn't have any children himself. He could organise visas and things. The Spanish man was much older than the Indian man, perhaps around seventy years of age.

It seemed really strange to me and it made me worried. Nobody had ever said they wanted to adopt me before. And anyway, I already had a father.

He said we would talk about school tomorrow. Then the Spanish man attempted to give me another big tip. It was feeling wrong to keep taking so much money, and I was still suspicious, so I said, "You've given me too much money already. From now on I'll bring you to your hotel for free. I can't take any more." But again he shoved the tip into my pocket and said, "We'll see you tomorrow."

It was all very confusing. On the one hand, I was really happy. I was getting big tips of five hundred or a thousand rupees a day. I had never had so much money in my life. But on the other hand I was starting to become scared about it all. I was thinking, is there some big reason for this? What will they want in return? Each evening when they came out of the Indiana, I could tell that they had been drinking alcohol with their food. I could smell it on their breath. I really didn't trust people who had been drinking alcohol, and I never believed anything that they said. People become different when they drink liquor. So I thought, 'I'll wait and see what happens in the next days, but I'll be sure to not spend any of the money. I'll keep hold of it all. Then, if they want something in return for it, I'll give all the money back to them.'

On the 4th day at around 8 or 9 p.m., I was sitting near to the Indiana, waiting for them again. They arrived in a taxi and after saying hello to me, and asking me to wait for them, they went inside to eat.

Later, on the way to their hotel, the Spanish man started asking me lots of questions. They both had blankets with them. Jaipur gets pretty cold at night in the winter. He said "Don't you feel cold?" So I said, "When I'm cycling the rickshaw I don't feel cold because it's hard work. But I feel cold when I'm not working." Then he asked, "Do you have a mother and father?" So I told him my mother had died of TB when I was very small, but I had a father. When we arrived at the hotel, he said, "We have talked to a charity, and they can help you. My business supports them. They'll come to meet you tomorrow at the Indiana at around 8 or 9 o'clock. We'll talk to them. Will you be able to come?" So I said yes. When I refused a big tip again, they put it in my pocket.

Cycling back towards the Indiana, I was starting to feel really scared. I wondered if something big was going to happen that would change my life. It was feeling like I might have no control over anything if rich people started to make decisions for me. Maybe a charity would organise things for me and I'd have to do what they said. It was very difficult to say no to important people. I knew I couldn't go to school. Also I was worried that they might try to put me in some kind of institution, like that orphanage in Agra.

The next morning, since I suddenly had lots of money, I took a shower and washed my clothes. In the afternoon, I locked my rickshaw and walked to the Muslim colony where we used to live when I was a little kid, where Yellow Dog had bitten me in the street. I used to walk there when Aunty controlled my life, to get away from it all. That was the last place that I had ever felt really happy. I stayed there talking with my old Muslim friends and neighbours. Time passed quickly, and I sort of forgot that I had agreed to meet the people from the charity. Or maybe I didn't really forget it. It wasn't deliberate, but maybe I was so worried about it that I pushed it out of my head.

After I walked back, the security guard at the Indiana called me over. He was very angry. He said a group of important-looking people from a charity had come to see me. They waited a long time, but they were gone now. I was relieved to hear that. The Indian and Spanish men were eating inside. They had asked him to tell them when I arrived. He told a waiter to take a message to them and they came outside.

The Spanish man said, "Where were you? Our friends from the charity came and we waited for you for hours. They had prepared all the paperwork and forms that they needed to help you."

I said, "Sir, I'm really sorry. I had completely forgotten that

I had to meet you. I walked a long way to meet some old friends. Whenever I am worried or sad, I go to meet them, because they make me feel better."

He wasn't angry about it. He said, "Well, never mind, let's wait until tomorrow. I'll phone them tonight, and then tomorrow we can all talk." So I said, "Okay sir." Then they went back inside to finish eating.

Later when I dropped them at their hotel, the Indian man gave me a big tip. I tried to refuse, but he said, "You have to take it. It's my boss's money. I work for him and he told me to give it to you." Then the Spanish man said, "You're a very nice boy. And your future could be very bright." Although it was a good thing to hear, nobody had ever told me before that my future could be bright. I didn't believe it either. But I said I would meet them again the next day.

On the 6th day I expected the same things would happen at the last days, but when I was sitting outside, the Indian man came out of the Indiana early. There was a taxi waiting for him. He said, "I have to go to Delhi for an urgent business meeting. My flight is in few hours. But our charity team will contact you soon. I have given them all your details and the address of the Indiana." And then he said, "My boss has asked me to speak with your father before I leave." So I said, "That's my father lying on the floor over there." My papa was really very drunk. Too drunk to even stand up. And as we walked towards him he started shouting. Not at us, just shouting about nothing. Angry at the universe. So I explained to the man that when my father was drunk he shouted a lot for no reason. I felt embarrassed, but he just said, "Oh, okay, so that's your father." He told me he didn't need to speak with papa. He said his team would keep him informed, and then he got into his taxi.

Later, when I was taking the Spanish man to his hotel he spotted an unusual-looking rickshaw in the street. He asked me to stop so he could look at it. Then he said, "How much does a rickshaw cost?" I knew that a second-hand one was about five thousand rupees and a new one about eight thousand, but I wasn't sure how to say the numbers in English. So I said, "Fivety thousand ... fifty rupees ... five ...thousand." He took out his mobile phone and asked me to type the amount. It was a very complicated phone. A BlackBerry I think they were called. And I didn't know what to do with it. I'd never even used a simple mobile phone before and I wasn't sure how many zeros there were in five thousand. I told him a friend of mine spoke very good Spanish. I could get him to translate for us tomorrow.

He asked me to eat dinner with him at the Indiana the next day at 9 o'clock. I said I would, but I was very nervous about it. The next day, I took a shower and put on clean clothes, but even when I arrived outside the restaurant, I wasn't sure if I would go in. I was hiding behind a tree and I watched him arrive in a taxi and look around for me before going inside.

The thing was, I had never eaten in an expensive restaurant like that before. I thought, 'what can I order?' and 'what will we talk about?' His English was not much better than mine. It didn't seem like we could have a proper conversation.

I was still wondering what I should do when a waiter came outside. I saw the security guard pointing to me. The waiter said to me, "You have to come inside. The Spanish man has promised me a big tip if I bring you with me." I told him I was scared, but he said, "All the restaurant waiters and staff know you Naresh. They'll handle it. It'll be fine." So I went with him.

When I sat down, the Spanish man asked, "Why are you scared?" I tried to explain, but my English wasn't good enough. And I felt really uncomfortable.

The manager asked what I would like to eat, so I ordered *dal roti*, which is the simplest thing they had. That's lentils with chapattis. It's what they usually cook to feed the staff. I ate it very quickly, but the Spanish man was eating slowly and sipping beer. So when I was finished, I told him I would wait for him outside.

I know he thought it was strange that I was so scared. But at least he had seen now that I wouldn't make a good adopted son.

I had asked my friend Shankar to be there. He sold Rajasthani puppets on the street. Somehow he had learned to speak very good Spanish.

When the Spanish man came out, he asked Shankar how much a rickshaw cost. So I told Shankar, "A new one comes for 8,000 or 8,500 rupees, and a second-hand one for 5,000 to 5,500." Shankar spoke with him a while and then he said, "He told me he was only interested in the price because he saw an unusual rickshaw yesterday. He says he's definitely not planning to buy you one. I asked him."

I tried not to show it, but of course, I was really disappointed. I was hoping he might be thinking about buying me my own rickshaw. A new rickshaw was about one hundred and fifty US dollars at the time. Maybe that's just what the Spanish man spent in a restaurant each day, but it was an impossible amount of money for me. Owning my own rickshaw would change my life. I would be free from paying rent. Every rickshaw puller wanted to own one, but almost nobody did.

When I dropped the Spanish man at his hotel, I sat outside for a while thinking. Then I saw him watching me from his window. He waved and quickly came outside again. He said, "I have to go to Delhi by car tomorrow for something urgent." He tapped a finger on his watch and said, "Can you be here at 9 a.m. tomorrow morning?" Again I became nervous, because I thought, maybe he wants to take me to Delhi with him. So I asked him why. He said, "Before I leave, I want to buy you a rickshaw. You will need to come here on foot. And bring along the guy who speaks Spanish." Then he hugged me and went inside again.

I don't really like people hugging me, but on the way home I was jumping for joy. And I cycled back to the Indiana at full speed because I needed to find Shankar before he went home. I was just in time, because he had packed his puppet bag and was ready to go. Shankar agreed to come with me the next day to translate, if I would buy him a bottle of English wine.

When we arrived at the hotel the next morning we were a bit late and the Spanish man was already waiting outside, standing near to a big foreign car. For the first time, he really looked like a rich businessman. It was like the mafia was waiting for us. He had a big dangerous-looking guy wearing a dark suit and sunglasses standing behind him, like the bodyguards do in Bollywood films. I had never seen anything like that before in real life.

We drove to a workshop in the Pink City where they make and repair rickshaws. The only one that was ready to be sold was what all the rickshaw pullers call a *naag raj riksha*. That means a snake rickshaw. They have a fixed metal canopy over the passenger seat. They're called that because from the side the shape is a bit like a cobra that's about to attack.

Snake rickshaws are very heavy, and because the metal canopy is heavy they can fall over easily unless the rickshaw puller is a bit heavy as well. I was small and thin. Also, if you go over a hole in the street, any tall passengers bounce on the seat and bang their head under the metal canopy. Every rickshaw puller knows that.

I had tried cycling a snake rickshaw a few times, and it was too difficult for me. There are lighter rickshaws with a folding canopy made of canvass. They're cheaper than snake rickshaws. But the shop didn't have one ready for sale at the time. The shop owner said he was repairing a second-hand one but it would take four or five days to get ready. So the Spanish man said, "I can't wait that long. I'm leaving today. So I'll buy the snake rickshaw if that's the only one available."

I knew the snake rickshaw would be too heavy for me, so I said, "No, that would only waste your money. I wouldn't be able to use it. We should forget about it."

He tried to convince me, but I told him again that I wouldn't be able to use it and so it would be a waste of his money. All the time Shankar was translating, but he was also telling me in Hindi, "Are you crazy? Take it. You can sell it when he goes to Delhi." But I told him to leave it because there was no point wasting money on a rickshaw that I couldn't drive.

Then the Spanish man said, "You really are such a stubborn boy. You never agree to anything!" So he spoke with the shop owner and placed an order for a lighter rickshaw. He paid cash for it, and gave me the receipt so I could pick it up later in the week. He said he couldn't drop us back at the Indiana because he was already late and he needed to get to Delhi for his meeting.

When we reached his car, he said, "Before I leave, I want to talk to you about a few things. I liked you from the very first day I met you, and I want to adopt you and give you a good life by taking you to Spain. I have nobody in Spain. I don't have a family, only a business partner. She lives with me, and I want you to come to Spain and live with us as well. As my son you would have an amazing life. I could give you everything you've ever wanted. But first, we need to find a hostel for you, so you can get off the streets and learn how to read and write. While you're there, I'll get my team to organise a passport and visa for you. I can make those things happen though my business. So you need to think carefully about this. Your father's life is already over because of the alcohol, and there's no future for you here. You need to leave your father behind and come to Spain with me. Think it over for a few days and let me know. This is my business card and it has my number on it. You can call me any time."

So I told him, "Thank you, but I don't need time to think about it. I could never leave my papa under any circumstances. He has raised me since my mother died, and we have always been there for each other, even in some very bad times. Now that my sister is married, I'm all that he has got left in the world. What would happen to him if I went away? Nobody else looks after him. If I'm lucky in the future, then I would love to come to Spain to visit you. But I could never leave my papa permanently."

When Shankar had finished translating, something happened that really shocked me. The Spanish man started to cry in the street. His bodyguard looked shocked as well. He hugged me and said, "I have never come across a child like you before. I wish you were my son. Maybe we'll meet again sometime, but I don't know when that will be. Enjoy your new rickshaw, and take care of your father and yourself." Then he got into his car and was driven away.

❖ ❖ ❖

Everybody was amazed when I showed up with my own rickshaw a few days later. And some were quite jealous. The rickshaw pullers were all saying things like, "It's not possible that some foreigner just gives you a rickshaw as a gift. Things like that don't happen."

When I handed my rented rickshaw back to its owner, he also didn't believe that a foreigner had simply given me a rickshaw, for no reason. But whatever they all believed, it was true.

❖ ❖ ❖

Less than two weeks later, when I was returning home at night, the security guard at the Indiana told me the Spanish man was back in Jaipur. He had left a message for me to come to his hotel. I went there straight away, but the lady in the reception told me he would be sleeping and I should come back tomorrow. Street kids aren't taken very seriously in expensive hotels. The next morning I went back. Again they wouldn't ring his room when I asked. The lady told me I should wait for him outside in the street.

A bit later he came outside carrying a book to help him translate things from Spanish into English, because sometimes he didn't know the English words for things. He told me he would be in Jaipur for just one day. He had come especially to see me and the new rickshaw. I had already had it decorated and it looked really cool. He took lots of photographs of the rickshaw and of me. He wanted me to take him around Jaipur for a few hours before dropping him off so he could return to Delhi.

While we were eating lunch he said, "I needed to know for sure that you really did pick up the rickshaw. I wondered if maybe it was a clever scam and you had taken the money instead. But now I'm convinced."

From all the big tips he had given me, I had also bought a simple mobile phone, my first ever. So I could give him my number. In India you have to have an ID to buy a SIM card. Than meant I needed to buy a second-hand SIM card from somebody who had an ID. But the card expired soon after. At that time the cheapest SIM cards only worked for a short period. So I had to get another second-hand card, and I lost the phone number I had given to my Spanish client.

◆ ◆ ◆

It may seem like a small thing to you – owning a rickshaw worth 100 dollars – but it changed my life in a very big way. For the first time, I didn't owe money to somebody every day. I became happier and more self-confident because I was free. And because I didn't need to pay rickshaw rent, for the first time I started to think that maybe I could find a room to live in, and move off the street.

My own rickshaw was beautiful, with blue frame and a comfortable red passenger seat. I decorated it and I had a radio with stereo speakers put into the back. When I played music on my radio, tourists would often smile and take photographs. And then I didn't have to try very hard, they wanted to be my passenger. I realised that positive things attract positive things, and positive people attract positive people.

A few months later my Spanish client suddenly showed

up again in Jaipur. He surprised me by coming to the Indiana Restaurant one evening. He had brought his friend with him who he had told me had been his business partner since the early days. They invited me to eat with them at the Indiana. This time I was not so afraid. We ate dinner together and talked a lot. His partner was younger than him. She was a Spanish lady of about sixty years of age and she spoke very good English. My Spanish client – his name was John Veeza – told me he had tried to phone me often. So I explained how I had lost my phone number because the SIM card had expired.

When I dropped them at their hotel, I asked when I would see them again. John said they would certainly be back in Jaipur soon. He wasn't sure exactly when, but he would contact me, or see me at the Indiana. When we said goodbye that evening, I didn't realise that I would never see him again. He never did come back.

After then, whenever I had a Spanish client, I always used to tell them that the man who gifted the rickshaw to me was Spanish. Sometimes they would tell me that 'John Veeza' didn't sound much like a Spanish name. I wasn't sure of the spelling because I couldn't read at all back in those days, and somehow I had lost the business card he had given me. Later, when clients had smart phones with them, I would ask them to try to find him on-line, but they never could. And years later, when I had learned to read and write a little, I tried hard to find him myself, but I never found a trace. It was like he had completely vanished.

John Veeza changed the direction of my life from downward to upward with the gift of that rickshaw. He had no reason to help me. There was nothing I could give him in return and he never asked for anything. Whenever I think of my past, I really miss him. I would like the opportunity to say thank you, and tell him how important he was in my life. If he is still alive, perhaps he will read this one day.

Chapter 8: Making foreign friends

I started to realise that being around foreigners was usually interesting and fun. I liked people from all countries, but especially people from Japan. They were always really kind to me, and we got along very well. I never understood why that was.

One day when I was sitting outside Niro's Restaurant on the M.I. Road, two Japanese girls came out. Their names were very similar. They were called Aiko and Akiko, and I couldn't remember who was who. Perhaps they were older than they looked, but I thought they were aged about eighteen or nineteen. I was around fifteen at the time, so they were not much older than me. And they were both very pretty.

They handed me their hotel card and asked me to take them there. On the way, I asked if they wanted my special sightseeing tour of Jaipur the next day. They said they would be leaving for Delhi the next day, but they asked if I could pick them up at 9 a.m. to take them to the train station.

The next day, when I dropped them at the station, they said they would buy their train tickets and then come back outside to pick up their luggage. It's really not a good idea to leave your bags with a stranger, but Japanese people usually trust everybody. So I kept all their bags in my rickshaw and waited while they went to buy their tickets.

More than an hour later, they came back outside. One of them said, "We need to go to a money changer. They won't take dollars or yen or even a credit card. They want us to pay cash with rupees, and we don't have enough." I explained that the money changer would be closed because it was Sunday. They wanted to go and try anyway, but of course, it was closed, and all the banks were closed too.

I had about fifteen hundred rupees saved in the box under the seat of my rickshaw, so I told them they could borrow that if they wanted. At first they refused, but I persuaded them to go and book their tickets for the next day. By then they had already missed their train. Buying a train ticket is probably quicker and easier in Japan than Jaipur. So they decided to spend an extra day in Jaipur and take the A.C. Volvo bus to Delhi instead of the train, because a bus ticket was easier to buy.

Then they said, "Let's go and eat breakfast together." I was very shy at that time, especially around pretty girls, and I felt uncomfortable going into fancy restaurants because my clothes were old and worn out. For some reason, they wanted to eat Chinese food for breakfast, but when we arrived at the restaurant, I told them to go inside, and I would wait for them outside.

The old rickshaw men had told me stories about the all the strange things Chinese people would eat, so I was afraid to try Chinese food. But those stupid stories were wrong, as usual, and I love Chinese food now. I have even been to Hong Kong once, and the food was great.

So they went inside, but they came straight back out. One of them said to me, "We can't eat like this without you. If you don't eat, then we won't eat either." They wouldn't listen to my objections. They said, "Why don't you take us wherever you would normally go, and we'll eat the food that you recommend." So I took them to a great *kachori-samosa* stall that I know. We each had a *kachori* and a *samosa*. The food at that stall is some of the best street food in Jaipur. They also sold *mirchi vada* there. In Rajasthan, those are big green *bhavnagri* peppers that are stuffed with potatoes and *garam masala* then battered and fried. You eat them with tomato chutney. I thought they would be too spicy for Japanese people, but they wanted to try those too, and we all agreed that they were fantastic. And we finished off with a sweet sticky *jalebi* each.

We spent the rest of the day roaming around together in

my rickshaw. They ate an amazing amount, although they were both very thin. They wanted to try everything. In the afternoon we went to see a film at the Golcha Cinema in the Pink City, carrying all their luggage inside with us. They made me sit in between them, and at one point in the film, when a girl changed her clothes behind a screen, they both put their hands over my eyes and said I shouldn't look because I was too young. They were really funny to be around.

In the evening I took them to the Indiana Restaurant so they could watch the Rajasthani dance while they ate, but they wouldn't go inside without me, not even when I told them that I would be given free food outside by the restaurant manager. All drivers who brought a client to the Indiana were given free food while they waited. So instead we ate chicken kebabs sitting on the kerb. And then they wanted to see the place where I slept in the street. I took them to my spot near the *chai* stall where I'd worked as a little kid.

They talked for a while in Japanese and then they asked me, "Do you know a good hotel or guest house where three of us could stay for one night?" So I took them to a few places, but nowhere would allow me to stay, and then they refused to stay there as well. Eventually we went back to their original hotel, but they also wouldn't allow me to stay. By then the Japanese girls were getting a bit angry about it. They said that in Japan, if you pay for a room, it's none of their business who stays there, and they could never discriminate against anybody. I explained that in India no decent hotel would allow a street boy without an ID to stay overnight.

There was no choice. They couldn't sleep in the street. So they took a room and I went home.

The next day, they planned to get a late bus, so I took them all over the city, stopping off at the best street food stalls and *dhabas*. They wanted to try everything, and they always made me decide what we would eat. So we had amazing *masala dosas* with coconut sauce from a street stall that I know. Later we ate *gol gappa*, which are crispy *puris* filled with potatoes, onion, and coriander, and *dahi patashi*, which are puris that they break open and fill with potatoes and yoghurt.

Before going to the bus station Aiko and Akiko each wrote me a letter in Japanese. I never did find out what those letters said. They got ruined during the monsoon season a couple of months later.

As their bus drove out of Sindhi Camp bus station, they both watched me through the window and started to cry. One of them passed me her watch out of the window and said I should wear it to remember her. I cried as well when I saw them leaving. We had swapped phone numbers, but in those days phone calls to Japan were extremely expensive, and so we lost touch. I wished I could have gone to Japan with them.

Perhaps you wonder how I could store a number in my mobile phone and know who it belonged to, because I couldn't read or write. I had to make up my own system. In those days I only had an old-fashioned keyboard phone. I used to use emojis or those little pictures of a car or a house, or sometimes a number like 123 or 000. Then I just needed to remember that the house picture was my friend Guddu, because I used to go to his parent's house when I was a little kid, or that 11 was the two Japanese girls, or that the policeman picture was the security guard at the Indiana. If you can't read, everything in your life is more difficult. I knew I needed to start to learn somehow.

◆ ◆ ◆

Then I had one of the biggest chances of my life so far. I spent a few days with a French client called Philippe. He was a lecturer at the University of Paris and a really nice person. We got along very well although I made him angry a few times because I made stupid mistakes. One day I tried to take him to the Amber fort. I had never been there before and I didn't know it was more than ten kilometres from the Pink City and mostly uphill. You can't do that in a cycle-rickshaw. So I wasted a lot of his time. But Philippe remained very kind to me.

On his last day in Jaipur, he said, "I have a surprise for you. I have got you enrolled in a school. I have been to speak with them. They are expecting you on Monday. Just take these papers with you. They won't ask you for anything else. Show them this form and tell them my name. I'll e-mail the rest to them. If there are any problems, then tell them that they should contact me." He had even stayed one extra day in Jaipur to arrange it all.

He had visited St Xavier's, a big private college not far from the Indiana. It was maybe the best school in Jaipur, and very expensive. It was a big building in its own grounds. But St Xavier's also had a charity school, just inside the gate, that poor kids could attend. That was paid for by donations from rich people. Philippe must have made a donation to get me in. Or perhaps it was because he was from Paris University.

You may think that was a great opportunity. And it should have been. On Monday morning I did try. I felt really shy walking in through the gate among all those rich kids in their perfectly clean school uniforms. I'd also stood outside a while and watched the charity kids arriving. They didn't have to wear uniforms, because uniforms are really expensive. Those kids were not from rich families, but they were arriving in autorickshaws or being dropped off in cars. There were no street kids among them. They were all kids who could take a shower every day, and had clean clothes to put on.

I was to be put in a group with children who were about five years of age who couldn't read yet, and I was around fifteen. I was much older than all the other charity kids. I had never been inside a place like that before, and I was feeling very uncomfortable. But there was something even more important than that. I knew I had a simple choice: I could either go to school and learn, or I could work and earn money to eat. I couldn't do both. I knew papa would never earn enough to keep the both of us and pay for his drink. So I walked out of St Xavier's on the first day, and I never went back.

About a year later, Philippe returned to Jaipur and he found me. He was disappointed that I never went to the school, but not angry about it. He said, "Why didn't you stick it out? It's a good, international school. They would have taught you really well." I also knew it was a missed opportunity. But it wasn't that simple. Kids should go to school, they shouldn't work. But for street kids like me, if they don't work, they starve.

It was impossible for me to explain that to Philippe. I apologised for wasting his money like that. But he has remained a good friend, and we are still in contact.

◆ ◆ ◆

I met so many foreigners who told me I needed to learn to read and write. I knew that my life would never improve if I couldn't read. But it was another Spanish client, called Raul, who made me decide to really do something about it.

Raul used to come to Jaipur often. He used to buy jewellery wholesale and sell it at his shop in Spain. Jaipur has a lot of gem dealers who sell rubies and sapphires, and there are workshops all over the city where they cut and polish them and turn them into jewellery.

One day Raul told me that if I learned to read and write he would start to teach me how to buy jewellery next time he came to India. Then when I knew what I was doing, he wouldn't need to spend so much money on flights to India. I could buy things for him and send them to Spain.

From that day I started thinking about how I could do this. I knew lots of the rickshaw pullers took teachers to school every morning. They were regular passengers. So I used to tell everybody, "If you know a teacher, can you ask them if they give private tuition? Tell them that a young rickshaw puller wants to take lessons for 1 or 2 hours in the evening or in the morning, whenever they have time. And he will pay whatever their fees are."

One rickshaw puller I knew, called Sanju, told me, "I know a family. It's a big Muslim family. Fifty or sixty of them live together in a house in the Pink City. I'll talk to them. There are many teachers in that family who teach in government schools and private schools."

I didn't really think Sanju would do anything, but I met him again a few days later and he said, "I talked to that Muslim family. There's a lady in the family who may be prepared to teach you. She's a teacher at a government school. She doesn't usually give private lessons, but she says she may have time to teach you in the evening. But first she wants to meet you." Sanju told me he would take me there the next day.

The next day I took a shower and put clean clothes on so I didn't make a bad impression, and I went there with Sanju. It was a big house with big rooms, and it was clear that a really a big family lived there. Perhaps eight or ten people lived in each room. Different generations of the same family. Sanju took me up to the roof, where there were 3 rooms, a big tin shed and also a kitchen. I was introduced to the entire family of the teacher. The teacher, who was called Pinky Madam, asked me about my past, and said, "Why do you want to study? By now you should already be in the 10th or 12th class."

I told her the truth about my past and how I lived now. Then she asked me if I could read and write in Hindi. I told her that I had learned little bits in the past, but I'd forgotten everything and that I could hardly read at all.

So she said, "Okay. From tomorrow onwards come to study from 7 to 8 in the evening. I'll only be able to teach you for one hour, because when I get home from school I have to do some household chores and also prepare lessons for the next day."

I was really happy. I said, "No problem Madam, I'll be here at 7 o'clock in the evening." When I asked her how much she would charge, she said, "I'll teach you for two hundred rupees a month." That's about three US dollars. Even I could save that amount in a month. Then she made me drink a cup of tea, and insisted that Sanju and I stayed to eat with her family.

The next day I took a shower again and I went there in the evening. I felt very shy going there alone, but when I asked Sanju to come with me, he said, "You're going there to study. That's something you've got to do yourself. So I'm not going to come with you."

I started to go every day. I used to walk there, because there was nowhere to park my rickshaw nearby. It used to take me about forty-five minutes to walk each way.

So Pinky Madam started to teach me how to read and write. And I started to get to know her whole family as well. Some Hindus will tell you negative things about Muslims. You shouldn't listen to them. They were a lovely family. I'm a Hindu, but that didn't matter to them. They were always sweet and friendly to me, and very respectful.

Each day, Pinky Madam used to give me homework to do. I used to do that when I didn't have a customer, under the shade of a tree. It's not easy to do homework when you don't have a home to do it in. Sometimes passers-by would watch me or ask why I was writing in a notebook, sitting in the back of a rickshaw. Some would even ask me directly, "What you are doing?" Indians are always curious to know what people are doing. So I used to say, "I've just started learning to read and write." Often they were shocked. They would say, "At your age? By now you should be in college!"

It was a big change for me. As the weeks went by I started understanding what was around me. For the first time in my life, street signs and shop signs started to make sense. I even started to learn how to read and write a little bit in English.

After a few months Pinky Madam refused to take any more money from me for the lessons. The whole family started considering me as a member of their household. I got to know everybody. When they needed a rickshaw, I would take them places for free, in exchange for my lessons. I didn't go there every evening, just two or three times a week when it was tourist season, but more often if there was no work.

There was one member of the family who became my favourite. She was kind to everybody and always smiling and happy. Everyone in the house used to call her *dadi.* That means grandmother. So I also started calling her *dadi* as well. She was the oldest member of the family, and she owned the house, although her husband was the head of the household and decided what happened. He used to be a *pahalwan* when he was young, but he'd given up treating people's bones a long time ago. After my lesson, I would always go downstairs to say hello to *dadi.*

Whenever there was a celebration in the house, or someone was getting married, *dadi* used to insist that I came as well. And whenever she had cooked a special dish she would call me to try some of it. I still visit *dadi* sometimes and we speak on the phone too. I also got to know her niece, who was the daughter of Pinky Madam's sister. Her name was Shiba. When I visited *dadi*, she would ask Shiba to make *chai* for me. If anybody was around, Shiba and I never spoke. And in a house with sixty people living in it, there is always somebody around. But secretly we used to send funny messages to one another on our mobile phones. We started arranging to meet sometimes in the park. That had to be kept top secret, because a Muslim girl is not allowed to be a friend of a Hindu boy.

My Spanish client, Raul, never came back to Jaipur, so I never learned how to buy gemstones. But we are Facebook friends now. And I'm grateful to him for the push that he gave me.

Chapter 9: The day the Pink City changed

Then one day, Jaipur changed forever. It was a Tuesday, the thirteenth of May, 2008. A day of terror for everybody.

A group of people hired bikes and cycle-rickshaws to deliver packages around the city. Those packages contained powerful bombs, full of scraps of metal and ball bearings. At about 7:30 in the evening, when the streets were very busy, the bombs all exploded together near to markets and temples.

Hundreds were hurt and about eighty people were killed. Nothing like that had ever happened before in Jaipur.

For days there were military police and soldiers everywhere, and there was a curfew each evening. A curfew is a big problem when you live on the street. It's illegal to be outside after a certain time, but where do you go?

Suddenly every rickshaw puller and street person was suspected of being a terrorist. Many roads were closed. In other places there were road blocks where the police were stopping rickshaws in the street, checking IDs, and looking for bombs. Anybody who didn't have an ID with them was taken to jail while the police investigated who they were. Many people who I knew were taken by the police. People who didn't have an ID at all were kept in jail. They said that some people without an ID might be illegal immigrants from Bangladesh who were pretending to be Indians, and they would be sent back to Bangladesh. We were all afraid. We used to hear the latest news from somebody who could read. They would read the newspaper out loud and we would all gather around them in the street to listen.

I became really scared, because I couldn't prove anything.

Not even that I was Indian. I had no ID at all. And if I was taken to jail, I didn't even have the phone number of a relative who could prove I was part of their family. I was too scared to go anywhere, so I just stayed next to my parked rickshaw near to the Indiana, and hoped the police didn't come. All the rickshaw pullers from the *chai* stall where I used to work stayed near to the *chai* stall for days, because they knew the *chai* boss would vouch for them if the police came.

When the curfew began in the evening, I would go and sit all night with the security guards just inside the grounds of the Jai Club. That was on private land, so it was OK to be there. If anybody asked who I was or what I was doing there, I knew for sure that the security guards would support me. They had all known me for years. Other street people had to hide inside derelict houses, or crouch all night behind walls.

A few days after the bombing, everything became a bit more normal again. The roads were opened and the curfew was lifted. I was still really afraid, but I had to earn some money, so I started cycling my rickshaw again.

Sometimes, when I was waiting outside a shop for passenger to return, people would be suspicious of me. I would see them cross over the road to get away from me. Sometimes they would come to me and ask, "Why are you waiting here?" So I used to tell them, "I'm waiting for my passenger. They're inside that shop." Then they would say, "OK, open the box under the passenger seat and let me look inside." I didn't want any trouble, so I used to let them to check the box. It only ever contained some clothes and soap, and my spare flip flops.

A friend of mine was injured in one of the blasts. He was a rickshaw puller of about 50 or 55 years of age. I met him a few weeks later when he was out of hospital. He told me he had been waiting for a passenger by the Hanuman temple near the Sanganeri Gate when a bomb had exploded nearby. He'd been pretty badly hurt, and his rickshaw was destroyed. But the government had given him a new rickshaw and few *lakhs* of rupees as compensation, so he was one of the lucky ones.

When the bombs exploded, all the rickshaw pullers who thought they were only being paid to deliver packages around the city were killed. They were victims like everybody else. It was not fair because everyone was blaming them as if they were the terrorists. The terrorists thought their aim was more important than people's lives. None of us even knew what their aim was. I still don't know. In any case, hurting and killing all those people didn't make anything better. It made things worse for everybody. It was like Jaipur had been a sleeping child who woke up as an angry adult.

That was when it finally hit me that I absolutely had to get some kind of ID card. I knew it would be a big problem for me for my whole life if I didn't.

◆ ◆ ◆

When things were calmer in Jaipur, I decided to go back to Ajmer and ask my *bua* again if she would help me to get an ID. She only needed to say that I lived in her house and let me borrow some bills. I explained to her how dangerous it had become for me. If there were any more problems in Jaipur, I was afraid that the police could put me in jail, or maybe even send me to Bangladesh if they didn't believe I was Indian.

Once again, my *bua* refused. Like the last time, she said, "I don't know what you get up to in Jaipur. What if you get into trouble? Then we would be held responsible." I did my best to persuade her. I said, "I'm like a son to you. We're family. Please help me. This is really important to me." But she didn't want to even talk about it.

I had planned to go to my sister's house to see if her husband could help. But I was so upset that I went straight back home to Jaipur. The big problem was, in order to get an ID, I needed to live legally in a room so I would have official bills with my name and address on them. But to rent a room legally, I needed an ID. It was a circle that went round and round.

◆ ◆ ◆

I started to ask advice from everybody. I knew there had to be a way out of the problem, but I would need to be really clever about it. It was not going to be easy. So I listened to what people had to say. Nobody suggested anything that would work.

Then I had a conversation with an LIC agent who worked for the Life Insurance Corporation of India. He use to drink *chai* at a stall behind Niros restaurant, and I'd known him for a long time. We were both drinking *chai* there one day, and we started talking.

He said, "Why don't you get an LIC insurance policy? If you have an accident, your family will get the benefit, and if you get sick you can get treated at the hospital for free." It didn't sound like much of an idea to me at first. It sounded like an insurance salesman trying to sell insurance to me.

It would cost 350 rupees a month, he told me. That was a lot of money for me to spend just on an insurance policy. But then he told me that with an LIC policy I could apply for a PAN card. You need a PAN card to pay income tax, but it's not a proof of ID. He said the tax people didn't care if you had a proper address or not, as long as you paid your taxes to them. And then, if I had a PAN card, I would be able to get bank account so I could pay the tax. The bank would use the address on the PAN card. He said he could apply for the policy, because that was his job, and he could also apply for the PAN card for me. He would use his own home address for the policy because you only needed a post address for that. Of course he would earn a commission, I knew that, and I would also need to pay him to do it all. But he was a good guy, and I knew I could trust him.

I thought about it for a while. It was going to be very complicated, but it seemed like my only chance, so I asked him to arrange the LIC policy for me. Just a week later it had already arrived. Then he applied for the PAN card. I paid him 200 rupees to fill-in the form, and to use his post address. About six weeks later he handed me my PAN card. He said, "Now you can go and open a bank account. You'll need to take along a guarantor whose account is already with that bank."

I asked my friend Sanju – the one who had introduced me to Pinky Madam – because I knew he had a bank account, and he agreed to go with me and act as guarantor at the bank. In no time at all I had a bank account as well. Step by step by step it was all starting to work. I was collecting things to prove my identity. It felt incredible.

I knew the next step was going to be the most difficult. I would need to rent a room illegally, get to know the landlord, and when he trusted me, ask him to help me get an ID using his electricity bill or something. Maybe I would need to pay him for his help. That was what my friend Ajay, the high-cast rickshaw boy had done. He'd told me about it. After the bomb blasts, when things got really dangerous for us all, he'd rented a room illegally, and now he had an ID card as well.

Ajay lived in an area of the Pink City where landlords weren't too worried about the rules or the law, as long as you paid your rent on time with cash. He spoke to his landlord, and then took me to meet him. I was taken to see a room on the top floor of the building. It was quite big, with red-painted walls, and it was completely empty, besides lots of dust and dirt everywhere. It would be expensive, at 900 rupees a month, but I had a regular client at that time who was living in Jaipur for a few months, and I had started saving quite a lot of money. I jumped at the chance. I paid a month's rent in advance, and I was given a key. It was the key to my first real home in more than ten years. It was the start of 2009 and I was about sixteen, I guess.

I was so excited about it. I used some of my savings to buy cooking equipment, a blanket, a mattress to sleep on, and an electric *punkah*. My room was on the top floor and so it got very hot because the sun was on the roof all day long. Maybe that was why it was empty. So I really needed that fan.

The first night sleeping in that big empty room was very strange for me. I think it was the first time I'd ever slept in a room alone, but I felt very, very happy. And I felt safe. There were no bugs, no rats, no traffic, and nobody could interfere with me while I was asleep. It was pretty quiet in the house most of the time, except in the morning. There was no tap in the house, so everybody had to fill buckets of water from a standpipe out in the street. All the neighbours too. Inside the Pink City walls they only switch the water on for about one hour each morning, so you can imagine how crazy that gets with people trying to collect buckets and pots of water before they switch the water off again. Rich people have a tank inside their house that fills up when the water is on, so they have water all day long.

I had to share a toilet with 6 families in the house, but that so was much better than having to use a public toilet in the street. In each of the other rooms, families of four or five people lived. Nobody had a bathroom. Most of the men would get washed outside their room just wearing their underpants and using a bucket of water. But the women would never do that. I was also too shy to do that, so I always got washed inside my room. That was messy, and I had to be careful that water didn't leak through the floor. Mostly I went to the public bathhouse to take a shower.

Indian people don't usually live alone, and it felt very strange for me to live alone. I really wanted to bring my papa there. It didn't feel right for me to sleep indoors while he was still sleeping in the street, but I was afraid he would drink and shout, and we would get kicked out by the owner.

Up to that point I hadn't told papa about any of it. When I told him I had rented a room, he agreed to come with me to stay there. But as soon as we reached the room he said, "I want to have a drink to celebrate this." From that day, he started drinking heavily, and I couldn't stop him. In the beginning it was OK, but after a couple of days he got out of control and started shouting again at night. Everybody in the house went to bed by around 10 o'clock, and then it got very quiet. They all complained to the landlord about the noise, and papa was told he had to leave, or we both had to leave. So papa moved back out onto the street.

After a couple of days I started feeling really guilty. So I locked the room and began sleeping in the street again, near to papa. Somebody had to make sure he didn't get into any trouble.

When he was not drunk, I tried to reason with him. I'd say, "You've got to stop this stupid drinking. You're getting too old for it now. You could just stay at home and rest, and let me take care of everything. If you don't, our lives are going to go in different directions. And I don't want that."

I tried really hard, but he wouldn't agree. So I decided that I had no choice but to live alone and leave papa on the street. This could be my only chance to change my life, and I couldn't allow papa's drinking to take it away. I knew that if I did, one day I would also be an old man, sleeping in the street, probably getting drunk every night as well to make my life seem better. I'd think back to the time when one decision could have changed everything, and I'd know exactly when that one mistake was made.

I cleaned all the dust and dirt out of the room and I moved back in.

I had bought a small gas ring and some pans and utensils. I'd always been interested in cooking, but I didn't know how to cook at all. I tried to cook rice for the first time. I didn't realise you had to add water before heating it. I went to market and bought cooking oil. I put some oil and dry rice into a pan, put the lid on, and started to heat it. After a couple of minutes the room was full of smoke and the rice was burned.

After that, early in the morning when I used to eat food at my favourite little *dhaba* at the side of the road, I used to watch closely how the ladies cooked parathas and chapattis. After watching them a few times, I took some flour home and slowly learned how to cook them myself. But I was lonely living alone in that big room, and I decided finally that whatever happened I would have to bring my papa home with me and make him stay.

Like I told you, at that time I was earning good money, and I had saved quite a lot. I had recently bought a second-hand rickshaw for my papa. One day I took him to my room, and when he was asleep, I went out, locked the door behind me, and secretly sold his rickshaw.

Papa was a serious addict, and I knew I needed to be really tough with him to break his addiction. So I started locking him in the room during the day while I went out to work. My room had a thick old door with a strong lock, and it was on the top floor, so there was really nothing he could do.

I told him, "If you want anything, food, milk, juice, or *beedis*, just ask me. But I'll only bring you one quarter bottle of wine each evening. The days of drinking four or five bottles of wine every night are over." I felt like I had become a stern father and he was a naughty child. He had no choice. He had no rickshaw now, so he had no way to earn money for himself. Also, by then his eyesight was becoming quite bad, so it was getting difficult for him to work, and he knew that. He got angry with me a lot, but he knew this was his very last chance. His choice was to live comfortably without alcohol and let me arrange everything, or die alone in the street one night.

◆ ◆ ◆

It wasn't always easy living there, but we were doing OK. I could pay the rent and buy food. Papa didn't drink, and he caused no big problems. I got to know the landlord, and I counted the months passing.

The simplest photo ID card you could get was a 'ration card.' The government gave those out to the poorest people. With a ration card you could buy things like oil, flour, and maize at a subsidized government shop for much less money than in normal shops.

After papa and I had lived there for about eight or nine months, I told the landlord that I needed to get a ration card to buy food. And to do that, I'd need him to sign a form to say I lived there. And I'd also need one of his electricity bills. He seemed quite annoyed about it. He said, "Why should I do that? I hardly even know you! What if you get into trouble? Then the police will come knocking on my door."

So I said, "But you helped my friend Ajay after he had lived here just a couple of weeks." Still he still refused. He said, "You'll need to live here a lot longer before I start to trust you."

Of course, although he was only a street boy like me, Ajay was still a high-caste Rajput. I guess that made a difference.

Ajay had paid a man called Pappu Bhai to arrange the card for him. Pappu Bhai worked together with a lawyer, and people who couldn't read or write paid them to apply for ration cards, even though the cards are issued by the government for free.

Pappu Bhai told me he still had a copy of the electricity bill that Ajay had used. If I gave him 1,200 rupees, he would use the same bill, and then get a local councillor to sign the form for me. He said the landlord wouldn't need to know anything about it. But I told him I didn't want to get a card that way. It would be illegal, and I wanted to do it properly, without telling lies or cheating people. He said, "You have no option apart from this." But I told him I'd prefer to wait and get to know the landlord, or find some other way to do it.

◆ ◆ ◆

Do you remember I told you about the guy in the dairy shop who was always making jokes? Remember, he was the one that made me quit my job at the *chai* stall after the owner had hit me because of one of his stupid jokes? I was very angry with him at the time, but I forgave him. I knew he was a good person really. He had just made a mistake. I used to call him Govind-uncle.

Over the years, I'd got to know him and his wife, Prakash-aunty, very well, and I often used to call-by to see them.

When I first started going to the dairy shop, I was quite afraid of Prakash-aunty. She was the opposite of her husband. She was very serious and strict-looking. She never made a joke, and she hated hearing people talking nonsense. In fact, she didn't speak to people very much at all.

She used to bring lunch for her husband and then look after the shop in the afternoon while he slept, because he used to start work at 4 or 5 in the morning, fetching milk and arranging things. When I knew she was at the shop, I used to avoid going there, because she was so scary and I thought she didn't like me. But sometimes I was asked to deliver milk to restaurants, and so I couldn't avoid her.

Now and then, Prakash-aunty would ask me to take her home in my rickshaw, and gradually I got to know her better. Then she would ask me more often to take her somewhere. As I got to know her, I found out she wasn't at all as stern as she seemed. That was a mask. Underneath the mask, she was a really kind person. When I would take her home, she always invited me inside, and insisted that I ate things and drank *chai* with her. She didn't speak much with people, but sometimes she would tell me the kind of things people don't usually say to anybody. She once told me that she didn't like her own name. Prakash is usually a man's name. When she was a little girl she had hated having a boy's name. She got used to it as she got older, but she still didn't really like it.

One time she asked where I was living now, and when I told her, she said, "Oh, I'm just so happy that you don't sleep in the street anymore." So I told her all about wanting to get a ration card, and how my landlord had refused to help. I told her, all he needed to do was let me borrow an electricity bill to take to the local councillor. Then the councillor would sign my form to prove I lived in the neighbourhood.

Prakash-aunty didn't say anything for a while, then few

minutes later she went to another room and returned with a pile of electricity bills and water bills. She said, "Naresh, we have known you for many years. You've become like a grandson to us. We own our own house and we have a successful business. We'll support you with whatever you need to get your ration card."

So I said, "Are you joking aunty? Even my own relatives have refused to help me." But she said, "Naresh, you know me better than that. I *never* make jokes!" She did make jokes, but people didn't understand them because she always sounded like she was being serious.

Although ration cards were free from the government, I decided to pay Pappu Bhai to fill in the form for me and arrange everything with his lawyer friend. It was too complicated for me to do on my own. We agreed that I would pay him six-hundred rupees in advance, and six-hundred when the card arrived.

When he was filling-in the form, he asked what my date of birth was. I told him I didn't know. So he said, "Well, you're going to have to choose a date then, because I need to write something here." I was around sixteen or seventeen at the time, but one guess was as good as another. I knew I would be safer if the card said I was an adult. So I chose a date of birth that made me an adult. For my birthday, I chose 14 January, the date of the yearly kite festival in Jaipur, *Makar Sankranti*.

◆ ◆ ◆

The day that Pappu Bhai handed me my ration card – my first official photo-ID – I looked into a mirror and swore to myself that I would never allow anybody to push me down again. I'd never allow the world to tell me I didn't really exist, or make me feel like I didn't matter. My life suddenly seemed different. I had an identity. I felt so happy that I could finally prove who I was, and that I was a citizen of India. I didn't feel so outside anymore.

The first thing I did was take my ration card to show to Prakash-aunty and Govind-uncle. I didn't have the words to thank them enough. In the following years, they really became like grandparents to me. They supported me to get all my other documents, like my driving license and passport. Once I had one official ID, getting the others was much easier.

In 2014, Prakash-aunty passed away. She had been ill for a while. I felt like I had lost my grandmother. Not long after that, Govind-uncle sold his shop and moved away from Jaipur to live with his daughter. I used to visit him sometimes. He too passed away recently.

Chapter 10: Little blue house on the edge of the desert

So that's my little story of how I became a street kid, and how I finally stopped being one. A lot has happened since those days. Perhaps I'll tell you about all that another time. But let me tell you why I decided to tell you my story right now.

Recently, things were going really well for me. My life was blessed. I had my own one-person business called Marigold Tuktuk and Car Tours, with a web site. People would book me to show them round Jaipur in my three-wheeled auto-rickshaw. My clients came from Japan, China, America, Europe, all over the world. I worked as their private driver while they stayed in Jaipur. My clients were mostly the unusual tourists. They were the ones who wanted to see the real Pink City, not just the famous sights. I could take them to drink *chai* or *lassi* in places they would never find or dare to go alone. I could show them the places that only the locals know, like small hidden temples, and places where you can eat the very best street food. I could take them to the amazing restaurant that sells only *dal bati churma,* or somewhere they could eat *ker sangri,* or get the best Rajasthani *thali*. Those dishes are only available in Rajasthan, and they are not like any Indian food you have ever had before.

So life was going fine. But then, at the start of 2020, my business ended overnight. The coronavirus had arrived in India. Jaipur was locked down, and there was another curfew. Tourists were banned from India, and the government stopped giving visas to people. So all of my bookings got cancelled.

But I'm one of the lucky ones. When the street people had nowhere to go when the lockdown came – all the *chai* boys, balloon sellers, rickshaw pullers, and bottle collectors – I had my own house, far outside crowded the Pink City. That's where most people were getting sick and dying at the start of the pandemic. This time, during the curfew, I had somewhere safe to stay indoors. When the daily wage-earners had no income, I had some money saved, so I could still buy food. I have always been one of the lucky ones.

I had never experienced anything like the lockdown. I had never had much free time before. I've always had to work, ever since I was a little kid. Suddenly there was nothing for me to do all day but stay home. I wondered if I could use all that spare time in a good way. So I decided to spend it telling you my story. I hope you have found it interesting. And perhaps if you ever visit India, you may understand a bit more about the lives of the street kids that you see, or the skinny old man who cycles your rickshaw and sleeps in the gutter. And you may be happy when you realise how great your own life is.

My life is also great now. I live in a lovely blue-painted house. When I moved to this colony it was very cheap here, because nobody lived nearby. Now other houses are being built in the area and it's becoming quite popular. But standing up on my flat roof, I can look out over the desert and the hills and see how beautiful it is here. I still have a lot of free time, because there aren't many tourists in India yet. So I've also started studying to take the junior school exams that I missed as a little kid. During the last couple of years my reading and writing have been improving a lot.

◆ ◆ ◆

My sister Raji still lives in Ajmer with her husband. She has a young son now. My *bua* still lives there too. And my papa lives together with me. He's almost completely blind now, and his eyes are getting worse by the day. The doctors say there is nothing they can do to help him. Soon he will be able to see nothing at all. But he's happy. He drinks *chai*, listens to music, sits in the shade and talks with the neighbours, and he sleeps a lot in his own bedroom. It's very quiet here outside the city. Sometimes I buy him *beedis* to smoke, but never, ever alcohol. He hasn't drunk a drop of wine or liquor for years.

In the monsoon season, when papa and I hear the rain crashing on our roof, we stay safe and dry inside our little blue house on the edge of the desert. And we remember how we used to stand all night in a shop doorway, when we slept on the streets of the Pink City.

Publisher's postscript

While *Pink City Kid* was being completed, prior to publication, Naresh got married to Shiba (the niece of Pinky Madam) who had transcribed his recordings. They now live together with Naresh's father and their young son Zane, in their little blue house on the edge of the desert.

Acknowledgements

I would like to thank some people for helping me with this book and throughout my life. My papa, Tikam Das Kishwani, my sister, Raji, and my grandmother. My teacher, Nigar Sultana (Pinky Madam). Gausiya Gauhar Shiba, who wrote down my Hindi voice recordings. Suneeta Pammnani who translated my story into English. Anneke Huigen, who edited the Dutch translation of the book, and Patrick Jered, who edited the English version. My old friend in Jaipur, Naresh. My old friend Guddu and his mother and father. Mr Gopi of the Gopi Samosa-Kachori Shop in Ajmer, who gave me a chance in life. The flower seller in Pushkar who saved me. Sanju, Pandit-ji, Satpal, Raul Mismo, John Veeza, and Philippe Cholet, and other friends in Jaipur and around the world who helped me in so many different ways. Some are mentioned in the story. Good things can come from from bad experiences. Even Aunty and the *chai* boss helped me find myself and change direction. And finally, I would like to thank Aunty Prakash Gupta and Uncle Govind Tikki Wal, who became grandparents to me; may you both rest in peace.

Naresh Kishwani, February, 2024

ABOUT THE AUTHOR

Naresh Kishwani

Naresh Kishwani spent most of his childhood and teenage years living as a street kid in Jaipur, India. For much of that time, he was trapped in some-or-other form of modern-day slavery.

He now runs his own small business – Marigold Tuktuk and Car Tours (https://marigoldtuktukandcartours.com/) – guiding international visitors around the real Jaipur, the city beyond the tourist sites.

Naresh lives in a house on the edge of the Thar desert, just outside Jaipur, together with his new partner Shiba, his young son, Zane, and his father. He is currently studying to improve his literacy, and plans to take the junior school examinations that he missed as a child. He is also working on the Hindi version of Pink City Kid.

Printed in Great Britain
by Amazon